D0917862

The Adjunct Faculty Handbook

Second Edition

The Adjunct Faculty Handbook

Second Edition

Lorri E. Cooper
Marymount University

Bryan A. Booth
University of Maryland University College

Editors

Los Angeles | London | New Delhi
Singapore | Washington DC

For information:

SAGE Publications, Inc.
2455 Teller Road
Thousand Oaks,
    California 91320
E-mail: order@sagepub.com

SAGE Publications India Pvt. Ltd.
B 1/I 1 Mohan Cooperative
    Industrial Area
Mathura Road, New Delhi 110 044
India

SAGE Publications Ltd.
1 Oliver's Yard
55 City Road
London EC1Y 1SP
United Kingdom

SAGE Publications Asia-Pacific Pte. Ltd.
33 Pekin Street #02-01
Far East Square
Singapore 048763

Printed in the United States of America

Library of Congress Cataloging-in-Publication Data

Cooper, Lorri.
The adjunct faculty handbook / editors, Lorri Cooper, Byan Booth.—2nd ed.
    p. cm.
Includes bibliographical references and index.
ISBN 978-1-4129-7519-3 (pbk.)
    1. College teaching—Handbooks, manuals, etc. 2. College teachers, Part-time—Handbooks, manuals, etc. I. Booth, Byan. II. Title.

LB2331.A37 2010
378.1′2—dc22

Printed on acid-free paper

10   11   12   13   14   10   9   8   7   6   5   4   3   2   1

Acquiring Editor:	Diane McDaniel
Editorial Assistant:	Ashley Conlon
Production Editor:	Brittany Bauhaus
Copy Editor:	Tina Hardy
Proofreader:	Dennis W. Webb
Indexer:	Rick Hurd
Typesetter:	C&M Digitals (P) Ltd.
Cover Designer:	Candice Harman
Marketing Manager:	Erica DeLuca

Brief Contents

Detailed Contents

Preface

Since the publication of *The Adjunct Faculty Handbook* in 1996, enrollment at institutions of higher education has greatly expanded. To keep up with these higher enrollments, institutions have increased the use of adjunct faculty to not only meet the volume demand of course offerings but also to

- Bring subject matter experts with real-world experience into the classroom
- Offer program specialties or minors particularly attractive to students
- Enhance the curriculum with innovative ideas and innovative teaching techniques
- Encourage faculty development through collaboration

The National Center for Education Statistics (NCES) reported that the percentage of adjunct faculty has risen from around 400,000 or 42% of total instructional faculty (NCES, 2007) to almost 670,000 or almost 49% of total instructional faculty (NCES, 2008). Sources such as the American Association of University Professors place the percentage of contingent faculty overall at 69% for two- and four-year institutions. Whether the figure is almost 50% or as high as 70% (dependent on classification of adjunct faculty members), there is no dispute as to the continuing institutional dependence on adjunct faculty by colleges and universities.

Adjunct faculty have multiple reference terms—adjunct, contingent faculty, part-time faculty—individually assigned by each institution of higher education. In their seminal book on "the invisible faculty," Gappa and Leslie (1993) formulated a typology to help define the motivation and lifestyle of adjunct faculty:

    I. *Specialist, Experts, Professionals:* Adjunct faculty work full-time in a profession and teach to remain connected to their professional network.

II. *Freelancers:* Adjunct faculty have more than one part-time position, or they may even have a full-time position at another college and teach a course for another.

III. *Career Enders:* Adjunct faculty may be near the end or at the end of their career and want to supplement their income or give back to the field and maintain contacts with like professionals.

IV. *Aspiring Academics:* Adjunct faculty may be early in their academic career, looking for experience and the possibility of a full-time academic position.

Since Gappa and Leslie's book, the increase in adjunct faculty has made all four types much more visible (and less "invisible") in higher education. The increased "professionalization" of adjunct faculty (e.g., unions and associations for adjunct faculty) has signaled to adjuncts, learning institutions, and to students the importance and value of adjunct faculty.

All types of adjunct faculty described and noted earlier, and throughout the book, can benefit from advice and approaches for teaching practices that enhance and increase effective learning. So, too, department chairs, course heads, program coordinators, and academic administrators are in need of guidelines, ideas, and suggestions for fostering engagement and professional development of adjunct faculty. The resulting effect of improving the entire adjunct experience for both adjuncts and administrators along with enhancing and developing skills among adjunct faculty will improve the overall quality of education provided for students. And *that* is the intent of this handbook.

Specifically, this handbook is designed to help the following:

- Full-time and part-time adjunct faculty (and general faculty) who want to improve their teaching and provide a richer learning environment for their students
- Program, department, and school administrators who hire and manage adjunct faculty and graduate student instructors
- Those in university centers of teaching excellence who provide resources for professional development and enrichment of teaching and learning (new to the second edition)

For the second edition, the foundational purpose of the edited text remained the same—a well-organized, easily understood, concise reference and guide, highlighting key information that instructors need to succeed in today's higher education teaching and learning environment. With the fundamental aim ensured, we next posed the obvious question: What has changed for adjunct faculty focused on teaching and learning since the publication of the first edition?

The obvious answer—**technology**. The rapid infusion and application of technology in our higher education classrooms of today, whether face-to-face or online, have significantly altered the expectations of students along with the range of designs for teaching methods. Thus, specific to the second edition, we have provided updated chapters on administrative guidelines, teaching and learning strategies, and evaluation of students. We have also introduced new and what we believe are essential and relevant topics concerning technology and professional development of adjunct faculty. Most distinctive, the handbook concludes with thought-leadership about the impact of future trends on the intersection of teaching and technology.

Some overlap of information occurs among the chapters as they were written by different authors and designed to stand alone for reference purposes. The structure of each chapter and style of writing also differ, due to the purpose of the chapter and the background of the author(s).

ORGANIZATION

Chapter 1, "Preparing to Teach: Considerations of Administration, Students, Technology, and Educational Results," covers essential administrative details and guidelines for ensuring successful teaching-learning experiences. Everything from signing a teaching contract to coordinating class meeting details to managing student administrative procedures is presented in narrative and checklist form.

Chapter 2, "Technology in Education," addresses both fundamental uses of technology in the classroom of today's "digital native" and differences adjunct faculty may expect to encounter whether teaching face-to-face or online. Examples of digital tools to assist in the development of media-rich teaching are described.

Chapter 3, "Environment of Learning: Connecting With Students," and Chapter 4, "Teaching Methods: Preparation and Application," present a critical and in-depth review of student learning theory and associated best teaching methods appropriate for any adjunct or full-time instructor. Most notable, here you will find richly detailed sections on dialogue as a teaching technique along with developing lesson plans.

Chapter 5, "Professional Development of the Adjunct Faculty," offers multiple suggestions and resources for professional development efforts of adjunct faculty and their commitment to excellent teaching. Ideas on institutional activities and low-cost resources are suggested for new teaching centers now established at most institutions.

Chapter 6, "Evaluation of Student Performance," reviews methods for evaluating student performance along with a discussion of academic integrity that highlights the impact of recent technology on violations and suggestions for prevention.

Chapter 7, "Future Trends: Network Technologies and Adjunct Faculty," discusses ways in which adjunct faculty can develop and grow their technology-based communication and networking skills to enable greater connections to students and colleagues. A model for choosing communication channels and networking modes is offered.

ANCILLARIES

For an electronic version of the Sample Lesson Plan in Appendix C and the Course Syllabus from Appendix D, please see the following URL: http://www.sagepub.com/cooperappendices.

REFERENCES

Gappa, J. M., & Leslie, D. W. (1993). *The invisible faculty. Improving the status of part-timers in higher education.* San Francisco: Jossey-Bass.

National Center for Education Statistics (NCES), U.S. Department of Education, Institute of Education Sciences. (2007). *Digest of education statistics.* Retrieved August 31, 2009, from http://nces.ed.gov/programs/digest/d08/tables/dt08_248.asp

National Center for Education Statistics (NCES), U.S. Department of Education, Institute of Education Sciences. (2008). *Digest of education statistics: 2008.* Retrieved August 31, 2009, from http://nces.ed.gov/programs/digest/d08/tables/dt08_245.asp?referrer=report

Note From the Editors of the First Edition

I was not surprised when we received a call from SAGE Publications to write a new edition for *The Adjunct Faculty Handbook,* a book my colleague, Dr. Neal Chalofsky, and I conceived and edited over 10 years ago.

Over that period of time, the entire adjunct faculty arena has exploded with numerous texts, journals, conventions, newsletters, and even union activity. We deans and chairs rely heavily on outside professionals to round out our schedules and degree plans. A nonpermanent, experienced workforce provides the kind of flexibility and outreach that today's universities demand, and managing and developing such extended faculty demands an entire set of guidelines and interactions.

Becoming an adjunct professor is now an actual career choice for experienced, degreed professionals who wish to expand their full-time jobs, extend their consulting work, stay in touch with research, passionately teach, or give back to the community. Certain adjunct faculty members have been able to cobble together a full-time slate of teaching by practicing at several universities at once. These adjunct faculty are highly prized as they establish relationships with various full-time faculty and students.

Unfortunately, when the call for a new edition came, Neal and I were knee-deep in other writing projects. We quickly realized there were many talented individuals who could take this project on. We interviewed a few outstanding professors and administrators and decided upon the wonderful team of Dr. Lorri Cooper and Dr. Bryan Booth. Their combined expertise in recent adjunct faculty hiring, development, and coaching made them uniquely perfect for this assignment.

Lorri and Bryan have done a stunning job of updating the original text with the latest methods, theories, and approaches in technology, methodology, measurement, personal development, and administrative concerns. This new edition should be read by all deans, chairs, program directors, adjunct faculty, and even full-time faculty. The skill sets are transferable to all academic populations. Creating a cohesive academic community, with all parties supporting and learning together, is the key.

Neal and I are disappointed that we could not work on this book ourselves, but we are delighted to introduce this new version. Happy teaching!

—Virginia Bianco-Mathis
—Neal Chalofsky

Acknowledgments

Becoming editors of the second edition of *The Adjunct Faculty Handbook* was only possible because of the foundational work done by the editors of the first edition: Virginia Bianco-Mathis and Neal Chalofsky. Stepping into their role was made easier due to the structure they established, the range and application of the topics chosen, and the tone set by outstanding contributors. Their book has endured and we hope to continue their success. We have been honored by both their belief in our capabilities and their support of our efforts.

Quite simply, the chapter contributors make this handbook. We benefitted from their expertise and their willingness to commit their time and understanding of important topics to and about adjunct faculty. They delivered chapters reflecting well-reasoned, thoughtful, knowledge areas integrated with practical advice and solutions grounded in their own experiences. We are delighted and thank them for everything they did.

Our universities have encouraged our time and energy with this book. In particular, we thank Jim Ryerson, dean, and Virginia Bianco-Mathis, management department chair, at the School of Business Administration, Marymount University; Michael Frank, dean, and Michael Evanchik, associate dean at the Graduate School of Management & Technology, University of Maryland University College.

We also wish to thank certain colleagues: at Marymount University, Catherine England, Amy Dufrane, and Ken Yusko, and at University of Maryland University College, Bryan's colleagues in the Doctor of Management Program. We *all* spent time as adjunct faculty prior to full-time careers in academia, engendering a special affection and commitment to the success of all adjuncts and a special appreciation for how adjuncts we work with today (and in the future) influence our own thinking and challenge us to strive for excellence as part of our contributions to our students' learning and our institutions' mission.

At SAGE, Diane McDaniel and Ashley Conlon were our mainstays through the formulation and production of the book. Thank you both for your editorial guidance (and correction!). We also thank our copy editor, Tina Hardy, for her precision and "caring" use of the red pen. Clearly, you are experienced at dealing with the best and sometimes challenging authors and editors.

Our families and close friends cheered us on with well wishes and the occasional "toast" as we completed each stage in the process and whenever we required an extra "push." Bryan offers special thanks to his wife Katharina and his children Alex and Emma for their support throughout. Lorri offers a thank-you to Chatsworth for his patience and understanding.

Finally . . . the best part of our endeavor has been the resulting collegial friendship we have built—freely sharing ideas and best practices, supporting one another in these and other administrative efforts—retaining our sense of humor through it all. True collaboration results in something much larger, more elegant, and rather different than the individual ideas, critiques, and visions offered throughout the process. This book has been such for us. We are most grateful for the resulting outcome.

—*Lorri E. Cooper*
—*Bryan A. Booth*

1

Preparing to Teach

Considerations of Administration, Students, Technology, and Educational Results

Lorri E. Cooper

This book begins by orienting adjunct faculty to their first challenge: navigating the details of university administration. In this chapter, Lorri Cooper provides pragmatic advice ranging from the specific to the general, from "Where and when does my class meet?" to "What resources and support are available to me and to my students?" Adjunct faculty may be practicing experts or they may be part-time academics employed by multiple institutions. No matter their background or purpose, all may be "challenged" by myriad administrative details to be addressed before teaching even begins!

This chapter provides checklists and guidelines for signing a teaching contract, coordinating class meeting details, and managing student administrative procedures. The chapter ends on an interesting and cautionary note with a matter-of-fact discussion on ethics and academic freedom along with an invitation to pause, even briefly, and reflect on preparing to excel in the classroom and how to produce worthy educational results.

All information provided in this chapter will be useful for new and continuing adjunct faculty. For university or program administrators, the chapter may serve as a foundational design both for planning adjunct orientations and as helpful guidelines in their adjunct development practice.

INTRODUCTION

This chapter provides an overview of activities and considerations for new and returning adjunct faculty prior to the launch of the teaching experience. From attending to administrative details required by programs, academic departments, and universities, to various components of student administration, to planning and finding support for classroom activities, explanations and suggestions are covered throughout the chapter. As adjunct faculty are part of the professoriate and thus have responsibilities for upholding and fostering ethical standards in their classrooms and at their institutions, details of these standards are given. Finally, an invitation to pause and reflect about delivering excellence in the classroom and what is required to produce worthy educational results is offered at the end of the chapter.

UNIVERSITY AND PROGRAM ADMINISTRATION

The relationship between adjunct faculty and institutions of higher education varies and is anything but predictable. Some setups are very organized and the adjunct faculty will be supported and recognized. Others are "sink or swim" situations in which an adjunct may be left to navigate the myriad of administrative systems unique to colleges and universities.

Most adjunct faculty can tell interesting stories of how they were hired and their first few teaching experiences. Exploring the following questions with your academic coordinator is a key first step in the process:

- What is the interviewing process? Will I be required to make a presentation or submit a sample lesson plan?
- How are decisions made concerning salary, title, and schedule? By whom?
- Will there be a formal acceptance letter and/or contract? When will this be received?
- What criteria are used for hiring and determining pay, title, and increases?
- What is the title structure for adjunct faculty (instructor, assistant adjunct, associate adjunct, etc.)?
- How is salary paid?
- When and how will communication be made concerning selection, schedule, class size, online or in-class location, class roster, and course materials?

Once hired, your next step is likely to be some type of orientation, possibly attending a scheduled session for adjunct or new faculty or directions for accessing information through a web document. Here you will be provided details on basic "how-to's," from obtaining an e-mail account and access to online systems (e.g., Blackboard, Sakai, Moodle) to navigating the campus and gaining physical access to campus buildings, including the assigned academic department and office space, if provided. If you will be teaching online, similar information is provided, usually with more detail on accessing all parts of the institution electronically. It is important in this process to also discover the varied provisions and locations of all available academic and student services including the library, instructional technology services and support, and student counseling centers.

Finally, there is what may be a valuable incentive and a significant reason why you may have felt encouraged to become an adjunct faculty member: institutional support for your development as a classroom or online teacher. The range of resources available for this purpose varies by institution and includes a spectrum from simple administrative help to coaching and mentorship programs, invitations to development seminars, access to on-campus teaching centers, communications provided to specifically support teaching and/or adjunct faculty, and awards and recognition lunches or dinners. Such access and active participation serve to create a sense of belonging to the academic community and reinforce commitment and quality.

If the institutional environment is less supportive or one with limited teaching support resources, you are encouraged to take a more proactive, resourceful, and creative approach. Suggestions include seeking out relationships with other department faculty or the department chair, perhaps reaching out to someone who has taught the course in the past or is teaching another section of the course, or demonstrating a willingness to share not only teaching materials but also your particular expertise through developing a unique lesson plan or offering to visit as a class guest speaker. Any efforts toward exhibiting a willingness to engage will be appreciated and recognized.

STUDENT ADMINISTRATION

For planning purposes and information (students will ask!), familiarize yourself with the university's registration procedure and dates. A general knowledge will be most helpful. As for your particular class, find out the dates for drop/add and whether a signature or approval is required of you. Sometimes students may ask you how late registration is conducted. Be prepared. Before the class begins, you will receive an enrollment roster and at some point, you will likely be required to submit a reconciled roster validating the accuracy of students enrolled. In addition, some institutions will direct you to use the roster as part of a required attendance policy.

Next is the all-important grades. What is the grading system used by the university? Are you required to file a midterm grade? When, where, and how must your final grades be turned in? This knowledge will have an effect on the timing of any final assignments completed by your students and your availability to grade them. What are the provisions and deadlines for a grade of "Incomplete" as well as for changing a grade?

Lastly, come student course evaluations. Student experiences and perceptions of the course are key tools not only for the advancement and development of your teaching style but also for the program director or department chair responsible for the program or degree in which the course is placed. Become familiar with the form and the process so that you may encourage students to provide the valuable feedback. After the course is completed, demonstrate your interest and willingness to improve by initiating a meeting with your university coordinator to review the results. You may further your engagement with the institution by preparing suggestions for improving the course based on your experience and the course evaluations. Some institutions may also offer midcourse behavioral observation questionnaires designed to provide you with "How am I doing?" feedback, allowing you to make changes appropriate to the experience of the students and the intended content of the course. Take advantage of this if available; it truly makes a difference in the overall course evaluation.

Preparing to Teach

Whether teaching face-to-face or online, adjunct faculty hope to begin their first class confident in their knowledge of the subject matter and in their ability to dazzle a room full of willing and talented students with their impressive teaching style. Before this occurs, however, the adjunct faculty must spend advance time attending to certain details that will ensure a successful beginning to every class.

The remainder of this chapter takes you through a series of questions to resolve before you actually start teaching. As you read through the guidelines and questions, you are encouraged to consider what is particular to your situation and record additional items for discovery on your own.

PLANNING AND SUPPORT

Syllabus

A syllabus is the foundational document for any course and serves as a guide for students about course format, requirements, and any particular administrative issues or points. It is the one best place to cover as much information as possible and the one place to which students continually refer through the course.

Some institutions may provide a template to be followed; others may leave the design and format to the adjunct faculty with directions to insert university statements on special needs accommodations, assessment, and academic integrity.

In either circumstance, pertinent information on the syllabus includes the following:

- A description or overview of the course
- Objectives: what the students will learn or be able to do upon successful completion
- Course materials such as textbooks, cases, journal readings, newspapers
- Methods of teaching: what the students can expect to experience in the classroom
- Descriptions of course requirements along with evaluation or grading information
- Information on how students may contact you and when you are available, which is the most important

In addition, you may consider adding helpful academic information, such as where students may access services at the institution to help them succeed academically (writing centers, advising centers, etc.), along with useful information about library access and support, especially if relevant course materials are on reserve. If the course has virtual elements (or if the entire course is online), information about support offered from the university's instructional technology group (HelpDesk) will be key.

Course Materials

Reading and preparation materials you will assign students for the course may range from the traditional textbook to journal or newspaper articles to simulations or other electronic media. It is possible the department in which you teach will select course materials intended for purchase by students. Whether you or your department, knowing who is responsible for coordinating an order at the bookstore and when the bookstore is available to your students will be helpful. This same information will be vital if you are responsible for selecting texts and other materials. Remember, students are quite adept at price comparison, thus they may request assigned textbook information prior to the beginning of class in order to consult availability and pricing at varied online retailers (e.g., Amazon, Barnes & Noble, halftext.com, etc.).

As you decide the scope of assignments for students, consider the resources available to them; knowledge of the library will be essential to your planning process. What materials does the library have on the particular subject matter? What assistance does the library offer students in their research process? How available is the library to you and your students? If necessary, what is the procedure for placing materials on reserve?

Finally, there is the matter of administrative support. It will be worthwhile to discover any type of support available in your department and what arrangements are necessary. The support may range from assistance with preparing copies and handouts for your course, arranging any particular classroom space or technical requirements, to possibly some research assistance with finding and preparing supplemental reading material.

Classroom Setting

If your course requires a classroom setting where you and the students are face-to-face, then for planning purposes and to help relieve any "first-night jitters," arrange to visit the classroom (or similar setting) in which you will be teaching. This gives you advance information on whether the room will need rearranging to accommodate your teaching style or special students, as well as familiarity with parking, restrooms, snack availability, and your general location. It also gives you the opportunity to visualize which instructional media forms are available or possible.

To begin, is the building in which you will conduct class sessions located on or off campus? Are parking facilities available? Are you required to have a sticker? (If so, where do you obtain one?) If parking is some distance from the classroom location, is there a shuttle available? What are the hours of operation? Are there any personal safety concerns about returning to your car after class? Are the classroom and the building accessible for all students? On the basis of your enrolled students list, will there be any requirements for special accommodations in the classroom?

Where are the restrooms and water fountains located? What are the locations and hours of operation of sources of snacks, drinks, or meals? If any problems should arise, how can security be contacted, and where are they located? Finding the answers to these questions may seem administrative and outside your concerns for teaching. But this is part of your planning process, and you can be sure that students will ask these same questions and more because you are accessible to them.

As for the classroom proper, will the standard arrangement accommodate your teaching style? Is it possible to have a different arrangement? Is there a policy that prohibits food and drink in the classroom? If you conduct group exercises in class, are there separate, small-group meeting spaces available nearby?

Must they be reserved prior to your class meeting? If some or all of your course activities require the use of labs, where are they located and how do you arrange to schedule them? What standard equipment is provided in the classroom? If you have some particular need for multimedia equipment or specific technology, whom do you contact for arrangement and assistance?

If your classroom "space" is virtual or you have some online component scheduled for your course, you have a different, yet similar, set of discoveries to make beyond developing your pedagogy for teaching online. How do you and the students access the electronic course platform, also known as a course (or learning) management system? (BlackBoard is popular.) At what point do students have access, especially newly admitted students? Will students access electronic-only copies of files or will hard copies be sent to them? Does the university have a protocol or standard for electronic use or learning material? How will you and the students access training on how to interact with the technology and navigate the course platform? Is there any specific software you and the students must purchase? Although it is likely the institution has protocols and varied sources for guidance and support, you are the students' central point of contact for the course and they will look to you first for answers and guidance. Be prepared!

ETHICS AND ACADEMIC FREEDOM

Every profession has ethical standards, and the professoriate is no exception. Adjunct faculty members represent the same model to students and the outside world as any full-time professor. The difference may be they have no responsibilities for faculty governance or service to the community. But as for any matter concerning students and the institution, the same ethical standards apply.

The institution's standard of academic freedom implies that along with your freedom to teach and pursue scholarly work, as an adjunct faculty member, you have the responsibility to represent yourself and your views accurately, both in and outside the classroom. This responsibility demands that when you are stating your beliefs and ideas, you make it clear that these are yours and not those of the institution. Likewise, you have the responsibility of accurately portraying your relationship with the university as that of adjunct faculty, not professor.

Within the realm of the classroom and relationships with the students, there is a whole other set of ethical standards. In the classroom, you have the responsibility of ensuring students' freedom to learn. First, you must protect students' freedom of speech: As part of the learning process, all students should be encouraged to express themselves and their ideas. Students must realize, however, that along with the freedom comes responsibility, and you may find yourself as arbiter in the classroom when the speech becomes harmful toward others. Awareness of your institution's policy concerning free speech is vital (Cahn, 1986).

Second, you must protect students' right to privacy. Private conversations between you and a student are confidential; so are your comments on any written work and any grades given. Third, you must protect students' right to due process, within both your classroom and the institution. And fourth, you must foster honest academic conduct. This involves not only representing yourself and your views appropriately but also exhibiting professional standards that protect the integrity of your course and protect honest students. Consulting the university's policy for dealing with academic misconduct is important.

Selection of course content and course materials is also an area in which ethical standards apply. Whatever you choose must be valid and credible with a clearly defined purpose. Be careful not to present materials that exclusively support your ideas and views, and do not present as final truth an idea that may still be undergoing scholarly debate. You have a responsibility to inform students that other views exist in a manner that does not distort or misrepresent those modified or opposing ideas. You have an obligation to guide students through their own scholarly pursuit, wherever it may lead them and you.

Another area in which you must be aware of the power and responsibility of your faculty position is that of assessing student learning and commenting on student work, both on papers and in recommendation letters. As an adjunct faculty member, you have the responsibility to design assessment instruments and testing procedures that do not allow any one student or group of students an unfair advantage. As the instructor, you are the person responsible for protecting student honesty and avoiding any violation of the integrity of the test. If a research paper is the required assignment, remember students put time, effort, and a part of themselves into each paper they prepare. Criticisms and comments should be constructive and encouraging, and if possible, designing a rubric to share with students enables you to demonstrate both expectations and consistency when grading. On occasion, you may receive student requests for recommendations or letters of reference. Writing these requires a certain finesse: An accurate portrayal of the student's performance abilities is the goal, yet inflation of these is sometimes the result. Consult with your department head or dean for guidance.

Finally, there is the issue of friendship. As a teacher in the classroom you have the responsibility of not only treating each student fairly but maintaining the appearance of impartiality. Favoring a particular student or group of students, however tempting or natural it may seem, compromises every student's learning process by raising questions of performance based on ability. Students observing such inappropriate friendships may begin to doubt your credibility, thereby weakening your ability to model scholarly behavior and serve effectively in an advisory role. Almost all schools have policies prohibiting sexual harassment. This helps ensure that student, faculty, and staff may work and learn in an environment conducive to intellectual, professional, and social development. Be aware of the operative policy at your respective college or university, as well as the formal grievance procedure for resolving such complaints.

You are human, and the profession of teaching is full of passion. Effective teaching demands the use of your emotions and knowledge plus your ability to deliberate and judge each student with impartiality. Do not compromise yourself or your standards.

REFLECTION ON TEACHING

Attending to all the administrative preparation details noted earlier in the chapter (and detailed in Appendix A) requires considerable time and accomplishes fundamentals necessary in the preparation to teach. Yet equally important is a commitment to set aside some time for reflection about excellence in the classroom. The reflection is not so much about your goals and objectives for the course and the students but rather more about the larger questions of teaching: How do you prepare to excel? How do you aim to produce worthy educational results?

Ken Bain's *What the Best College Teachers Do* (2004) is an excellent resource or "guide" for this endeavor. Bain and his colleagues undertook a study of outstanding professors to determine just what kinds of excellence produced important educational results in their students. Throughout the book, Bain centers on one question of outstanding teachers: *How did their teaching create or foster sustained and substantial influence on the ways students think, act, and feel?*

One conclusion from the study in particular is worthy of reflection and consideration. It centers on responses from the selected best college teachers to the question, "How Do They Prepare to Teach?" Rather than responding to the standard logistics of their course, number of students, meetings, classroom space, and so forth, these college teachers began more with considerations of student learning objectives, using rich lines of inquiry to design the entire course experience.

In the chapter on "preparing to teach," Bain (2004) offered questions that invite considered reflection of what is necessary to *create* an engaging, successful *learning* environment. (Create is the key defining term.) Most notable among the 13 questions posed are the following:

- What big questions will my course help students answer or what skills, abilities, or qualities will it help them develop, and how will I encourage my students' interest in these questions and abilities?
- How will I create a natural critical learning environment in which I embed the skills and information I wish to teach in assignments (questions and tasks) that students will find fascinating—authentic tasks that will arouse curiosity, challenge students to rethink their assumptions and examine their mental models of reality?
- How will I create a safe environment in which students can try, fail, receive feedback, and try again?
- How will I confront my students with conflicting problems (maybe even conflicting claims about the truth) and encourage them to grapple (perhaps collaboratively) with the issues?
- How will I communicate with students in a way that will keep them thinking? (Bain, 2004, pp. 50–58)

Reflection is a time-considered art. It is more than simple daydreaming. In reflection, the mind's thoughts are turned or fixed on some subject with deep, serious consideration. Reflection has elements of wonder, analysis, synthesis, and, most often, struggle. Time devoted to reflection about designing for excellence in the course and the production of worthy education results, coupled with fundamental beliefs and passions about the subject matter, create definition and purpose for adjunct faculty who aspire to deliver engagement and learning in the classroom.

CONCLUSION

Details, explanations, and suggestions on the range of considerations for preparing to teach covered in Chapter 1 are vital to the success of adjunct (and full-time) faculty. They may also be helpful as guidelines for academic coordinators and directors of university teaching centers committed to not only high levels of faculty engagement but also to fostering the professional development of adjunct faculty.

REFERENCES

Bain, K. (2004). *What the best college teachers do.* Cambridge, MA: Harvard University Press.

Cahn, S. (1986). *Saints and scamps: Ethics in academia.* Totowa, NJ: Rowman & Littlefield.

2

Technology in Education

Theodore E. Stone

Beginning with an intriguing look into the classroom of the "digital native" (students born into a technology-rich world), Theodore Stone invites "digital immigrants" (those born before the digital revolution) to look at their classrooms through a different lens and become more effective using technology in teaching. Citing evidence that learning in a media-rich, technology-rich classroom increases student satisfaction and improves student performance, Stone leads the reader through basic steps when teaching face-to-face—from determining exactly what is available in the classroom (projectors, computers, electronic teaching podium) or the building (Internet capability, laptops, data projector)—to the adjunct's most important communication tool, e-mail—to using digital media and web-based resources to enhance the learning experience.

In the section "Beyond the Basics," use of technology expands to encompass considerations of teaching online or web-based courses and hybrid courses (combination of face-to-face and online). "Web 2.0," a concept to describe the shift of web resources from static pages to an interactive and collaborative medium, is something which adjunct faculty may use to support classroom activities as well as provide opportunities for students to interact with content and apply its concepts in collaborative projects. Uniquely in his section on blogs, wikis, twitter, and texting, Stone offers concise and understandable explanations and examples of these technological tools known to have considerable appeal to students.

Finally, under the heading of "Distance Learning and the Adjunct Faculty," Stone argues that if adjunct faculty seek to become highly valued members of the academic community, they must not only become familiar with technologies

> technnologies available, but they must also prepare to teach in the Course Management System (or Learning Management System) of their institution. These systems (Blackboard, Web CT, and Angel are most common) have a number of products that support the online classroom environment. In addition, development of a library of digital learning objects, otherwise known as a professor's multimedia tool kit, is detailed.

Introduction

Many adjunct faculty find that arriving at a contemporary college classroom to teach can be an intimidating prospect for a whole host of reasons. Educational technology, and how it is changing teaching, is certainly at the top of the list for many. The ubiquitous presence of technology—at the front of the classroom and in the hands of the students—creates a very different teaching landscape compared to only a few years ago. To see this for yourself, try this little experiment: Walk into any lecture hall and look around a few minutes before the start of a lecture. Students are wearing earphones listening to mp3 players, mobile telephones are ringing, some students are typing text messages with their thumbs while others are pulling laptop computers out of their backpacks. Do you think a chalkboard and overhead projector will suffice to teach this crowd? Maybe. But maybe they have different expectations of what it means to learn in a modern college or university setting.

Welcome to the classroom of the *digital native*. Some believe that there has been a fundamental shift in recent years with the arrival of digital technology in education (Prensky, 2001). The students are digital natives; they have been born in a world that is technology rich, and they cannot remember a time when there wasn't a World Wide Web. And many of the professors standing in front of the classroom to teach them are *digital immigrants*, those who were born before the digital revolution and who have adapted to the changing technology-rich environment; some have adapted better than others.

If you are concerned about how you can more effectively use technology when you teach in a college classroom, then this chapter will be of help. It sets out to look at what some of the research says about teaching with technology and what that means for the typical adjunct professor or lecturer coming onto a campus to teach. The chapter examines basic options for education technology as well as what to expect in the high-end technology-rich classroom. The chapter also discusses differences between teaching in a face-to-face class, teaching in an online class, and teaching in a hybrid class, which is a combination of the two. Finally, the chapter describes some digital tools—tools that are free or practically free—that can help you develop media-rich teaching components for delivering instruction online or face-to-face.

THE FACE-TO-FACE TEACHING EXPERIENCE

For most adjunct faculty, the primary venue of instruction remains the traditional classroom on a college campus, whether that is a small classroom or a large lecture hall. Many colleges and universities have expanded locations off campus where courses are offered, so that often adjunct faculty are assigned to teach courses at these sites, such as high schools (on evenings and weekends), higher education centers (sites where multiple colleges and universities share classroom space), and even military bases. But whether you are teaching at a campus classroom or at a classroom that is off campus, you need to take into account what students expect from the classroom experience with you.

SO WHAT DO STUDENTS REALLY WANT?

Evidently, even modest applications of technology in a classroom can improve the student learning experience. In a 2004 study (Speaker, 2004), researchers examined student expectations for learning in a media-rich environment in a college classroom. More than 150 undergraduate students were surveyed to see whether the instructor's use of multimedia and other technology affected students' course decisions. The technology was not very sophisticated. The instructors used PowerPoint, overhead images, VHS/DVD presentations, and the Internet. The researchers found that students, not surprisingly, favored the use of technology; they reported that it improved their learning experience, and they perceived professors who used technology when they taught were easier to understand.

Students, some more than others, often bring expectations to learning with technology at a college or university. Those expectations of technology affect their attitude toward the learning experience (George & Sleeth, 1996). Interesting to note, research has shown significant differences in expectation among students based upon departmental affiliation. For example, a marketing or management major might come to class expecting a high level of multimedia, whereas an economics major may not. The differences in expectations caused the students to perceive the same class differently.

Overall, there is ample evidence that learning in a media-rich, technology-rich classroom not only increased student satisfaction, but also improved student performance (Gaytan & Slate, 2002). A consensus is emerging that learning is improved through more active learning on the part of the student, stimulated by visual cues and audio cues. And bringing media-rich resources into the classroom provides benefits to the faculty, as well. For example, when incorporating technology into the lectures and class presentations, faculty tend to refresh their class materials, discover more effective ways to communicate the materials, use new forms of teaching, and increase student sense of ownership in the class research.

It is important to keep in mind that in any given class of students, there will be a range of learning styles that has an impact on how students will perceive content. Learning style is related to how a learner prefers to learn (but preference should not be confused with ability; that is, if a student prefers active, hands-on learning from an interactive computer simulation, that does not mean he or she cannot learn from listening to a traditional lecture.) One model focuses on four continuums of learning styles: sensing versus intuitive, visual versus verbal, active versus reflective, and sequential versus holistic (Choi, Lee, & Jung, 2008).

SETTING UP THE BASICS

The first step when taking on an adjunct teaching assignment is to find out where the classroom in which you will be teaching is located (or if you will be teaching in an online classroom; more on that later in this chapter). More often than not, you will receive your teaching assignment a few months before you know the specific room to which you will be assigned. In fact, room assignments are typically made very late in the scheduling cycle at many colleges and universities, so you may not find out your room location until just before the start of the semester. But even if you do not know the exact room, your academic administrator or department chair can likely tell you if you will be teaching on campus or off campus. If off campus, he or she should be able to tell you the facility you will be teaching in, such as a higher education center, a high school, or some other locale.

Once you know the general location, you will be able to either visit a few classrooms at that locale or ask your department chair or academic administrator a few pertinent questions about the technology in the classroom:

- What technology is standard in the classrooms at this location (e.g., television monitor/VCR, overhead projector, projection screen, etc.)?

- Some classrooms have computers mounted in a teaching podium and which is connected to a data projector. Do the classrooms at the assigned teaching location have this type of technology or will instructors need to bring their own computers and projectors?
- Is the Internet available in the classroom, either by wired or wireless Ethernet? If it is available, does an instructor require a login and password to be authenticated? If so, where can an instructor go to get a login and password? (Remember: A login and password at one location, such as on campus, will likely be different than for an off-campus location.)
- If there is a computer network jack on the wall (for wired Ethernet), it doesn't necessarily mean that jack is "live." Who is the computer technology contact at the location where the instructor will be teaching in case technical support is needed? Ask for the evening and weekend contact numbers for technical support, because this is when you will likely be teaching as an adjunct professor.

Laptop and Data Projector

If you are assigned to teach at an off-campus location, you will more typically need to bring your own laptop and data projector if you want to use these as part of your basic technology setup (this will be the case for many classrooms on campus, as well). Many colleges and universities have audiovisual (AV) centers where faculty members are permitted to check out computers and data projectors for their classrooms. Each college has its own policy for the terms and length of time for borrowing. Some colleges will permit a faculty member to borrow equipment for an entire semester. Others have much briefer terms for lending. In any case, you will want to know where to go borrow the equipment and what terms and conditions to expect.

When borrowing equipment, it is advisable to ask the AV specialist to show you how to set up the equipment. This is a good idea because

- It allows you to ascertain the condition of the equipment and to verify that it is working and functioning normally (e.g., the bulb in the projector lights up; pins are not broken off cable connectors, etc.).
- It also allows you to verify that all components are present and accounted for (e.g., cables, power supplies, etc., are there).
- It provides a good opportunity to discuss with the AV specialists the types of activities you'll be doing with the technology. For example, do you plan to just show PowerPoint presentations or do you plan to use multimedia? If you plan to show a DVD in class on the computer, for

example, you can verify that the DVD is compatible with the equipment you will borrow. You can also make sure you have additional equipment you might need, such as an audio cable to go from the computer to the projector (for sound, if needed).

You cannot be too careful in this area. I have seen one experienced adjunct faculty borrow a data projector and laptop computer from the campus AV center for a class where students were going to be delivering high-stakes presentations that night. All the students had developed PowerPoint presentations; many of them planned to show additional resources with their presentations, including DVDs and other media clips that they needed to play through the computer. When the faculty member arrived at the classroom, she discovered that the AC power cord for the data projector was missing. The students were livid at the instructor and it was reflected in the student evaluations of the instructor at the end of the course.

Remember to look over the equipment carefully for any preexisting damage, because you'll be expected to sign it out. It doesn't hurt to get contact information for the AV department in case you have a question later.

E-Mail

More than any other, e-mail is the adjunct faculty member's most important communication tool. This is especially true because the adjunct instructor will not likely have an office or telephone on campus; thus he or she will not be able to keep regular face-to-face office hours for students, as would be the case with full-time faculty. In essence, the e-mail address becomes the adjunct faculty's virtual office. Thus it is important to keep in mind some important considerations:

1. Many colleges and universities offer their adjunct faculty accounts on the campus e-mail system (many of these institutions require that adjuncts use the campus e-mail for all academic business and e-correspondence.) If the college where you teach offers a campus e-mail address, it is a best practice to use it. Having a campus e-mail address allows you to keep all your academic e-mail in one location. And simply put, it looks more professional to have a campus e-mail address. If you do not have access to a campus e-mail address, you should consider setting up a special e-mail address on one of the free e-mail services (such as gmail). Select a name

that underscores for your students that this is a professional account, such as professor.jones@gmail.com or something similar.

2. Good e-mail etiquette is a critical component of being an adjunct faculty member. Because you are only on campus when you teach, e-mail will be the primary way for your students to initiate having a chat with you, one-on-one.

Remember to do the following:

- Check your e-mail regularly for your class. Some schools recommend checking three times per week. It may be better to check it at least once per day, and depending what is going on during the semester, perhaps more than once per day.
- If you have a campus e-mail address, use it when communicating with students and campus personnel.
- Whatever e-mail address you use, either a campus address or one you have set up just for your academic affairs, make sure your students know it. Put it with your contact information on your syllabus.
- When you give your students your e-mail address, make sure they know how quickly you plan to respond to them, whether that be within 6 hours or 48 hours. (This is important for students to know. If a student has an urgent problem, he or she will need to know how quickly you plan to respond. Otherwise, you may be inundated by a flood of frantic e-mails from the student.)

Digital Resources in the Classroom

For many adjunct faculty, using a computer and data projector will be an important part of how they will want to enhance a lecture or presentation. The most common way to do this is to use presentation software. PowerPoint, the presentation software component of Microsoft Office, is almost ubiquitous on college campuses. It is a very practical tool for enhancing presentations for instructors. More important, students expect to have access to PowerPoint if they are asked to give class presentations. If you are using a campus computer in your classroom, there is a high likelihood that PowerPoint is available. If it is not, there are free and open-source alternatives. For example, one alternative is Sun's OpenOffice. Similar to Microsoft Office, it is an office software suite that includes, among other tools, presentation software that can also read and display PowerPoint presentations. It is available for free download from openoffice.org. Another free alternative is Google Documents (or Google Docs), freely available to anyone with a free gmail account, available from gmail.com. Google Docs provides a suite of office tools online, in addition to online storage for the documents you create. Included in the online software suite is a presentation tool that allows a user to create and show a presentation. It also supports uploading and displaying preexisting PowerPoint presentations. Just remember, when using the Google Docs applications, access to the Internet will be required.

Many modern textbooks provide resources for the course instructor, which include chapter-by-chapter or module-by-module presentations that are ready-made to be used in a lecture or presentation. These presentations are often distributed by CD-ROM or via the publisher's web site along with other instructional resources. Using these presentations as a foundation, the adjunct professor may modify or supplement them as is appropriate.

Web-Based Resources

Of course, if the Internet is available in your classroom, then web-based resources are easy to bring into your classroom, whether they are basic web pages with graphics or media-rich elements such as videos from YouTube. There are comprehensive web sites that make it easy to find resources to bring into your classroom. For example, if you need to emphasize and amplify a historical reference in a lecture, there are sites that have created links to hundreds of museums around the world, so it is possible to bring in images of artwork and artifacts that enrich your presentation (Reissman, 2009).

Original Media

The classroom experience should not be merely a rehash of what the students read in their textbook or find on their own on the Internet. It should add a value that is framed by the professor's knowledge and experience. Creating original media and bringing authentic resources into the classroom is one way to do that. It has never been easier to create original media to bring into class to enhance the experience for your students. For example, I had a colleague who taught accounting, normally a dry and straightforward subject. But during the era of the Enron scandal, he found that there was an opportunity for a real-time case study to frame the accounting topics being covered in the text. To create these resources, he used his computer, an inexpensive telephone-recording microphone from Radio Shack, and Audacity, which was free, open-source recording software available from source-forge.net. With this setup, he recorded telephone interviews with various Chief Financial Officers from around the United States and Canada. He then introduced those interviews at appropriate times during the semester to amplify points made in the chapter for the week or in his lecture. It provided the foundation for rich discussions in his class and brought a value to his classroom that the students would not have otherwise been able to experience. (*nota bene:* The professor in this case could have used a simple tape recorder for recording the guest presenters, but he wanted to have the ability to make the recording available online for his students.)

Voice over Internet Protocol (VoIP) and Live Guest Lecturers

There are a number of Voice over Internet Protocol (VoIP) technologies that allow for voice communication and even video conferencing communication over the Internet. Free software programs such as Skype (skype.com) allow computer-to-computer voice communication at no charge. All that is required is an Internet connection in the classroom, a microphone, and speakers (a camera is optional) at both ends of the connection. This makes it possible to bring in live guest presenters into the classroom from anywhere in the world. Students are able to engage in a question-and-answer session with the guest speaker after a presentation, increasing the value to the classroom experience.

BEYOND THE BASICS

Although the basic classroom, with chalkboard and overhead projector, is still the dominant mode of instructional delivery on the college campus, one can find more and more high-end, technology-rich classrooms around campus. These technology-enhanced classrooms are attractively designed though expensive to build (hence not every classroom is so equipped). But even technology-rich classrooms are not all equal. People who have studied classroom design understand how a room design can encourage or constrain different types of teaching styles and learning styles (Hunley & Schaller, 2009). Classrooms that have fixed seating in a theater-style room may encourage the professor to give traditional lectures; rooms with movable seating make it easier for students to engage in small-group collaboration. What do some of these high-end, technology-rich classrooms look like and what types of technology are these classrooms equipped with? Some colleges and universities are establishing technology standards for their classrooms. Here are two examples:

Example No. 1: UCSC. The University of California, Santa Cruz (UCSC) has developed guidelines for the design and construction of classrooms at their university (Burnett, Wagner, Gyorkos, & Horn, 2003). In developing the guidelines, the university consulted with experts in the field of acoustics, ergonomics, and audio technology.

The UCSC guidelines take into account several aspects for the design of new classrooms and the renovation of old classrooms. In its guidelines, UCSC specifies standards for general classroom characteristics that might support teaching and learning in a media-rich environment. These include fixtures and furniture; lighting systems; cabling, telephone, and network outlets; media systems; and for larger classrooms and for lecture halls, projection booths are specified.

Interestingly, the UCSC guidelines take into consideration the convergence of distance education with face-to-face learning (we discuss the issues of distance education and online education later in this chapter). The report states the following:

> Emerging communication technology throughout the next decade will continue to grow rapidly. A major trend of merging technologies in hybrid configurations combining microcomputer technology, video technology and networks will allow the functionality of online text and graphics with features of television production in new formats. . . . Classrooms that are programmed as convergence distance education sites require special consideration (UCSC Classroom Guidelines, 2003).

Example No. 2: UMCP. The University of Maryland at College Park (UMCP) also has a variety of technology-equipped classrooms (Clabaugh, 2004). At UMCP, technology has contributed to a renewed interest in classroom design as well as the idea that well-equipped instructional facilities are a component of recruiting and retaining students and faculty.

UMCP has three categories of classroom space: general purpose classrooms, seminar rooms, and lecture halls. In designing its classrooms, the university focuses not only on technology but also the setting of the technology, such as details on spatial design and layout for classrooms, proximity to hallways, doorways, water fountains, vending machines, and restrooms (for noise abatement issues.) UMCP has taken into account building systems such as lighting, HVAC, electrical, telecommunications, media resources, and other technology. It even has standards for paint quality (for reflectivity issues). The high-end, technology-rich classrooms have multiple data projectors and screens, multiple workstations for students, which can be projected on one screen while the instructor's screen is projected on another. UMCP also has special software for the class to support online small-group collaboration, consensus building, and polling in the class.

Gaining Access to the Technology-Rich Classrooms

If you think you want to teach in a technology-rich, media-rich classroom, there are a few steps you might want to follow (which vary from campus to campus) that can help you get your class assigned to one of these classrooms:

1. Scope out the classrooms available. Review the campus web site and ask your department chair what classrooms may be available. Check with the office of academic technology at your campus to see what is available. Ask for a tour of the rooms.

2. Find out what you need to do to gain access to the room. Some universities have a formal application process to complete, to use the technology-rich classroom. Others have a less formal process but still require formal requests from department chairs or deans.

3. Before you ask to have your class scheduled for a particular classroom, you'll need to find out how far in advance you'll need to ask. Most importantly, you'll need to think through why you want to teach in technology-rich, media-rich environment. How do you plan to use the technology if you have the opportunity? How will it help your students to master the content? How will the technology interact with how you teach and your students learn?

4. Find out what training is available. Most colleges and universities have staff development opportunities available for teaching with technology. It makes it easier to get assigned to teach in a technology-rich classroom if you've already been trained in how to effectively teach with the technology that is available to you.

HYBRID CLASSES, WEB 2.0, AND ONLINE LEARNING

Adjunct faculty members in a modern college or university setting are being asked by administrators to teach classes that are face-to-face, web-based/online, or some combination of these two, also known as hybrid classes (sometimes called blended classes). A good place to begin thinking about these three modalities of the modern college class is with working definitions:

- **Face-to-face courses** are those that are taught using traditional face-to-face methods without any online activities or materials. Most educators these days would also include **web-enhanced courses** in this category. Web-enhanced courses are those that are taught primarily as face-to-face classes but also have some supplemental online resources and activities. The supplemental online materials are supportive of, but not critical to, the outcomes of the course.
- **Hybrid courses** are those that combine both the face-to-face learning experience and the online learning experience to the point that one is indispensable without the other.
- **Online courses** are those that are taught entirely online and there is no face-to-face contact between professor and students.

RESOURCES FOR HYBRID COURSES

Because online technology is so pervasive on college campuses, it is sometimes difficult to distinguish the differences between a web-enhanced course and a hybrid course. Here are a few examples a new adjunct professor may want to think about. Many textbook publishers, such as McGraw-Hill, Pearson, and others, often create companion web sites for the textbooks; these sites serve to supplement the books' contents. The resources may include audio and video files, text-based resources, photographs, and low-stakes testing (that is, tests and quizzes that typically would count for a small part of a final grade. When students take these quizzes, typically the student grade is e-mailed to the instructor by the publisher's system.)

Most colleges and universities have Course Management Systems (CMSs) such as Moodle, Sakai, and Blackboard (we discuss these in more detail in the section on online learning later in this chapter). A CMS allows for the easy creation and management of online classrooms that are web accessible and are used in both hybrid and full online classes. Students in a hybrid class, which regularly meets face-to-face, may also be required to collaborate in small study groups on class projects. That collaboration typically would happen in an online classroom that would be set up for the course on the college's CMS. Students may also be required to go to the online components in the CMS to access class resources, supplementary materials, and media objects that are associated with and required for the class.

Some hybrid courses may also use a different type of software called web conferencing software. Web conferencing software supports meeting in real time on the World Wide Web; popular versions of this software include Adobe Connect, Elluminate, and Wimba Classroom. Hybrid classes that use web conferencing software often alternate between meeting face-to-face and online. This creates flexibility in the commuting schedule for the students and allows the students and instructor to share resources easily during the class time when they meet in a web conference. Web conferencing products allow for VoIP, video cameras, text chatting, PowerPoint presentations, and sharing computer desktops. Some have the ability for group activities such as instant polling. Most allow for the recording and archiving of the meetings. This permits students to revisit the sessions as a study tool.

If your college or university has a license for one of these products, you'll need to investigate procedures for gaining access, because these procedures differ from college to college. Check with your department chair or with the academic technology director. Faculty members will need an account to set up their meeting space; some universities require faculty to go through training before being issued an account.

Web 2.0 and the Classroom

Only a few years ago, the World Wide Web was something that was simply viewed, not interacted with. But in the age of Web 2.0, the World Wide Web is a vast communication medium that enables community and communication on a number of levels. Generic resources such as blogs and wikis and specific resources such as MySpace, Facebook, Twitter, and Google Docs allow everyone to read, write, publish, form communities, and collaborate over the Internet.

The term *Web 2.0* is not an official term of any organization associated with the development of the World Wide Web. Rather it is a concept to describe the shift of web resources from static pages to an interactive and collaborative medium, with a more fluid relationship between the user's desktop and resources and information available on the World Wide Web. With a host of Web 2.0 resources freely available, it is possible to create hybrid classroom experiences to support classroom activities as well as provide opportunities for students to interact with content and apply its concepts in collaborative projects. Although the technology is rapidly changing, it is worth considering how some of these Web 2.0 technologies can be used as part of a hybrid class. It is also worth noting that tools such as blogs and wikis are part of CMS platforms such as Moodle, which may be available on your campus. But many of these tools are available freely and can be brought to good use in a college classroom. See the following, for example:

- **Blogs**. Blogs are web logs, or public diaries, that, if the author desires, may accept comments from readers as well. If you are teaching a class to which you would like to introduce a Web 2.0 technology, a blog is an easy one. For example, the professor may use a blog for class announcements, assignments, due dates, and so forth. Student blogs, as assignments, can be very effective if students need opportunities to reflect on reading or experiences, such as in writing classes, art appreciation classes, or teacher education classes. Some instructors use blogs to survey students on what they found to have been difficult from the last class. That way they can use "just-in-time teaching" methodologies to change their lectures before the next class (Higdon & Topaz, 2009). If blogging software is not available on campus, there are free services such as blogger.com.
- **Wikis**. Wikis are collaborative web documents that may have multiple authors. Wikis have the ability to create an audit trail of the revisions of a document, so it is possible to look at a document's history to see what changes were made and by whom. Wikis are perfect for collaborative assignments and small-group projects. As with blogs, if they are not available in the CMS on your campus, or through the academic technology department, there are freely available wikis such as pbworks, over the Internet.
- **Twitter, texting, and instant messages**. Many students have embraced the ability to send brief messages and carry on conversations. In the hybrid class, the professor can use these tools as well. For example, Twitter.com is a free social messaging system that allows the user to send out a brief text message. Sending out such a message is known as "tweeting." Subscribers to the messages can receive them on computer or on mobile devices such as a telephone. A professor can tweet students to remind

them to read a chapter or that class will be held online instead of on campus. The professor's tweets can also be automatically posted to the professor's blog. Similarly, most students have mobile telephones. Text messages from the professor can be sent directly to students' phones, if the students desire (some students may simply prefer e-mail because they may incur charges when receiving text messages). And there are a number of instant message tools such as Yahoo! Messenger or AOL Instant Messenger. These are useful for virtual office hours and being available to students for quick questions when you are online.

Remember, give your students clear rules of how they should use the Web 2.0 tools for communicating with you, such as how may you be contacted and when.

DISTANCE LEARNING AND THE ADJUNCT FACULTY

As an adjunct faculty, it is more and more likely that you will be asked to teach in a distance learning environment, most likely in an exclusively online setting. For some universities, online learning has become their predominant mode of instructional delivery. For example, University of Maryland University College (UMUC) has become one of the largest public universities in the world as result of its growth in online learning. There are lots of reasons that online learning is increasing in popularity. In fact, there has been a convergence of several factors contributing to the growth of the online learning phenomenon. These include faster, more ubiquitous bandwidth; faster, better computers; and, a rapidly changing economy encouraging nontraditional adult learners who are already in the workplace to return to college. The needs of adult learners have been a significant driver in the growth of online learning. Adult learners, because of obligations to work and family, need an educational program they can access anytime, anywhere. This is precisely what online learning does best.

A survey of members of the American Association of Community Colleges (AACC) underscores how widespread and pervasive online learning has become for colleges and universities (Lokken, 2009). Growth in online enrollments was significant and the colleges were struggling to keep up. Among the chief concerns of the academic administrators were "finding dedicated qualified faculty" to teach online and "convincing faculty of the need to become capable technologically as more and more students demand that faculty use the technology they depend upon in everyday life" (Lokken, 2009, p. 2).

The message is clear for adjunct faculty. If you want to be a highly valued member of the academic community, familiarize yourself with the technology available to teach, not only the technology used in the face-to-face classrooms, but also in the online classrooms. Prepare yourself to teach in the CMS on your campus. Most colleges and universities offer training in how to teach online, not only the nuts and bolts of using the CMS software but also in the pedagogy of teaching online: best practices for engaging students in a learning environment that is inherently asynchronous. That is, students do not log into the classroom at the same time. Because of that, the skills required for engaging students and helping them to construct their understanding of the subject area are different.

A FEW WORDS ABOUT THE COURSE MANAGEMENT SYSTEM

As was noted earlier, each campus is likely to have a single CMS (also referred to occasionally as a Learning Management System). According to the survey of AACC institutions, the vast majority of community colleges use either Blackboard, Web CT, or Angel as the three most common CMSs. Web CT and Angel have been bought out by Blackboard, which is now the dominant CMS at colleges and universities. Other CMSs that may be available on campus include two open-source products: Moodle and Sakai. Desire2Learn and eCollege are other common commercial products. Some of the very large online universities, such as UMUC, may use their own CMS that has been developed on campus. In the case of UMUC, its CMS is called WebTycho.

The CMS is an important component in online learning because it is the classroom—the virtual campus—of the online learning experience. Instead of the classroom being built of bricks and mortar, the classroom is built of "clicks" and electrons. The different products all have similar features to engender and support the online classroom environment (WCET, n.d.). From a student-faculty perspective, these typically include the following:

- Discussion forums
- File exchange
- Online journal and notes
- Real-time chat
- Whiteboard
- Calendar and progress review
- Group work support

- Community networking
- Student portfolio
- Quizzing and testing
- Online gradebook
- Student tracking

Many experienced online faculty agree that there is a learning curve to mastering teaching skills in the online learning environment. There is also more pressure on the faculty member to be very well prepared for the semester at the start of the online class. And faculty members who are new to online teaching often say they miss the face-to-face experience. But experienced online faculty will agree that there are advantages. For example, "learning any time, any place," as occurs in online learning, also means teaching any time, any place. Like the student, the professor is freed from the limitations of a physical classroom. Also, as the experienced faculty member builds a library of digital learning objects, these resources not only enrich the online classroom, but they can be used for face-to-face and hybrid classes, as well.

THE ONLINE PROFESSOR'S MULTIMEDIA TOOL KIT

So how does an adjunct faculty member begin to develop a library of digital learning objects? It sounds as if it is a lot of effort, but there are some tools that are available for free, or nearly free, that can be very useful in producing learning objects. These form the foundation of a multimedia tool kit. These include (a few of these products were referenced earlier in the chapter) the following:

- *Skype* is free VoIP and video conferencing software that connects with other computers that also have Skype. For a small fee, it is easy to connect to any telephone as well. Of special interest to the online instructor, when Skype is used with a companion product, *Pamela*, it is possible to record the audio of a Skype conversation and save it as an mp3 file. More information on Skype is available at skype.com, and more information on *Pamela* is available from pamela.biz.
- *Audacity* is free open-source software for recording and editing sound files. It can be used to record directly from your computer. It can even be used in conjunction with Skype and Pamela for editing files recorded with those products. More information and software downloads are available from audacity.sourceforge.net.

- *Windows Media Encoder.* Every now and then it is useful to have a brief video of the professor, if only a head-and-shoulder shot. If you have a small USB camera and microphone attached to your computer, it is easy to record brief snippets of yourself. This is useful if you want to personalize the start of a conference or introduce your notes for a text-based lecture. Windows Media Encoder is available for any Windows-based computer, either bundled with the Windows operating system or available for free download from microsoft.com. Students need the Windows Media player. For those students who use a Macintosh, a download is available to enable them to play the file, which is in a .wmv format.
- *Jing* is a freely accessible tool that allows users to record an area from their computer desktop with audio narration and record the desktop capture to a Flash video file. This is very useful for quick software demonstrations or other demos that require a small bit of "show-and-tell" on a computer. The recordings are limited to only a few minutes, but that can be plenty of time for a quick demonstration. The software is available from jingproject.com.
- *Impatica* is a "one-trick pony" software product that works in conjunction with a PowerPoint presentation. PowerPoint has the ability to add audio narration and timings to the slides for creating a stand-alone presentation. The problem is that the file is very large and not Internetfriendly. Impatica takes that large PowerPoint presentation file and renders it down to a Java file (.jar file) that can be easily linked to a web site and played over the Internet. This is the only product on the list that is not free, though many colleges and universities have worked out site license agreements for faculty members. It is available from impatica.com.

CONCLUSION

This chapter began by exploring what students at colleges and universities want. They want the same thing that college administrators want: professors who are competent to use the technologies that the students depend upon in their everyday lives. Faculty who incorporate technology into their classroom are typically viewed as easier to understand by their students. On most campuses, there are plenty of opportunities to learn how to use the new technologies, whether that is for enhancing the face-to-face classroom experience, creating a hybrid learning environment, or teaching online. Not to embrace the new technologies is to miss opportunities as an adjunct professor to enhance your class.

REFERENCES

Burnett, H., Wagner, J., Gyorkos, G., & Horn, B. (2003, December 9). *Classroom guidelines for the design and construction of classrooms.* Retrieved January 7, 2010, from http://media.ucsc.edu/contact/UCSC_Classroom_Guidelines03.pdf

Choi, I., Lee, S. J., & Jung, J. W. (2008). Designing multimedia case-based instruction acommodating students' diverse learning styles. *Journal of Educational Multimedia and Hypermedia, 17*(1), 5–25.

Clabaugh, S. (2004). *Classroom design manual: Guidelines for designing, constructing, and renovating instructional spaces at the University of Maryland* (version 4.0). Retrieved January 12, 2010, from http://www.oit.umd.edu/tc/UM_Classroom_Design.pdf

Gaytan, J. A., & Slate, J. R. (2002). Multimedia and the college of business: A literature review. *Journal of Research on Technology in Education, 35*(2), 186–205.

George, G., & Sleeth, R. G. (1996). Technology-assisted instruction in business schools: Measured effects on student attitudes, expectations and performance. *International Journal of Instructional Media, 23*(3), 239–244.

Higdon, J., & Topaz, C. (2009). Blogs and wikis as instructional tools: A social software adaptation of just-in-time teaching. *College Teaching, 57*(2), 105–109.

Hunley, S., & Schaller, M. (2009, March/Arpil). Assessment: The key to creating spaces that promote learning. *EDUCAUSE Review, 44*(2), 26–34.

Lokken, F. (2009). *2008 distance education survey results: Tracking the impact of elearning at community colleges.* Washington, DC: Instructional Technology Council.

Prensky, M. (2001, October). Digital natives, digital immigrants. *On the Horizon, 9*(5), 1–6.

Reissman, R. (2009, February). Museums in the classroom. *Learning and Leading with Technology, 36*(5), 36–37.

Speaker, K. (2004). Student perspectives: Expectations of multimedia technology in a college literature class. *Reading Improvement, 41*(4), 241–254.

UCSC classroom guidelines for the design and construction of classrooms at the University of California, Santa Cruz. (2003). Retrieved November 18, 2009, from http://media.ucsc.edu/contact/UCSC_Classroom_Guidelines03.pdf

WCET. (n.d.). *EduTools course management system comparisons—Reborn.* Retrieved May 29, 2009, from WCET EduTools: http://edutools.com/static.jsp?pj=4&page=HOME

3

Environment of Learning

Connecting With Students

Cynthia H. Roman

In an attempt to move college and university faculty into the 21st century, Cynthia Roman not only offers a critical examination of traditional ways of teaching but also what adjunct faculty need to know about students' learning and what teaching methods are best. Using learning-centered teaching as a foundation, where the focus is on the student learning rather than what a faculty member does, she includes detailed explanations of how students become learners (including "adult" learners) and how to determine their readiness for learning.

Accompanied by sage advice for how any level of faculty may reach and relate to students, Roman distinctively provides expanded sections on the use of dialogue in the classroom—a powerful, skillful process of developing and applying critical thinking to learning conversation, and the fine art of questioning—teaching with carefully crafted questions and teaching students how to ask the right kinds of questions.

Chapter 3 closes with practical guides for learning strategies for the online classroom and establishing an environment for learning. A checklist for facilitating learning in groups is provided.

INTRODUCTION

In the 21st century, many college faculty are still using lecture as their primary teaching method and students are required to read massive amounts of text material. Students may need to memorize large amounts of course and text-book content, and multiple-choice testing is used to assess student recall of information. Faculty members may think these methods are just fine. After all, that is what they remember from their college days. But are these teaching methods really the best for student learning? What is wrong with traditional ways of teaching in today's college classroom? What does the adjunct faculty need to know about student learning and what teaching methods are the best? This chapter addresses all of these questions.

Traditional, faculty-centered approaches to learning do not work, if they ever did, because students

- Fail to become engaged with the material
- Memorize materials often without truly understanding their meaning
- Do not remember material they learned earlier
- Cannot apply concepts to solve problems
- Have more information available with technology assistance (Blumberg, 2004)

Learning-centered teaching is an approach that focuses more on student learning than on what the faculty is doing. It isn't one specific teaching method but embraces many different learning-centered approaches. According to Weimer (2002), there are five practices that need to change to achieve learning-centered teaching:

- What the student is learning (the content)
- How the student is learning (the processes)
- The conditions under which the student is learning
- Whether the student is retaining and applying the learning (the processes and purposes of evaluation)
- How current learning positions the student for future learning

Blumberg (2004) discussed the benefits to students of learning-centered education programs. Students who have engaged in learning-centered education programs know they need to learn and know how to learn. They have self-awareness of their own learning abilities and their particular process of gaining learning ability. They can retrieve and evaluate information more effectively.

They have become more responsible and informed citizens. They use knowledge to solve problems more effectively, and they can communicate their knowledge in real settings.

THEORIES OF STUDENT LEARNING

Today's adjunct faculty is faced with students who hold a wide variety of attitudes due to their diverse ages, backgrounds, experiences, and cultures. For the traditional 18- to 22-year-old students, their 13 to 15 years of school experience taught them that the teacher is the authority who makes most, if not all, the decisions related to the learning experience. The teacher tells the students what to do and how to do it. Students have little choice in what they learn and the teacher has the right answers. Grades are much more important than learning because grades differentiate who will go to college, which college they will attend, and who will get financial scholarships. It is no wonder that for this age range of students, they will do almost anything to ensure a high grade.

Two theories help explain how students see formal school learning. In entity theory (Dweck, 2000), students view intelligence and ability as fundamentally fixed and unchangeable. This is the predominant perspective found among high school and college students (Covington, 1992; Steinberg, 1996). For students who hold this belief about their learning in academic areas, failure becomes evidence of their incompetence and the rationale for withdrawing from a future challenge or endeavor. These students believe people either get it or they do not. On the other hand, incremental theory (Dweck, 2000) views intelligence and ability as changeable and malleable. Incremental theory suggests that failure can be seen as feedback to help in making changes. Covington (1992) suggested that faculty can use incremental theory as a framework to help students develop goals and adjust attitudes toward failure. Whereas entity theory inhibits learning, incremental theory promotes learning by viewing failure as an opportunity for goal setting and change.

STUDENTS' READINESS FOR LEARNING

Faculty regard the classroom as a place where interested students comprehend and challenge complex ideas. In reality, classes often consist of students eagerly taking notes, willing to memorize anything for the exam, missing the course's essence, and not engaging in the main ideas being discussed. This causes much frustration among faculty, both full-time and adjunct. They may ask, "What's wrong with my teaching? What's wrong with my students?"

William Perry (1970, 1981) developed a well-known model that suggests how students make sense out of information, theories, experiences, and opinions in the college classroom. The three descriptions that follow summarize many of the differences in student thinking as Perry described them. It is important to note that this model applies primarily to students between the ages of 18 and 25.

Dualistic students use discrete, concrete, and absolute categories to understand people, knowledge, and values. They tend to think of their role in terms of "right" answers and the role of the faculty as providing those answers. They have low tolerance for ambiguity.

Multiplistic students acknowledge that there are multiple perspectives to a given problem or topic. There can be more than one right answer. A typical multiplistic response might be this: "We are all entitled to our own opinions." However, these students are unable to evaluate each perspective adequately. Argumentation ends, or it is avoided with the multiplistic attitude.

Relativistic students see knowledge as relative to a particular frame of reference. They show a capacity for detachment and they look for the "big picture." They have the capacity to think about their own thinking. Frequently, by seeing alternative perspectives, they have difficulty making a decision. Authorities are seen as people who can and should be questioned.

Understanding the Perry model can help the adjunct faculty understand that student perspectives can be very different from faculty expectations. For example, a number of responses to an assignment might be appropriate and correct but a dualistic student might be disturbed by the idea of multiple answers. Academic study requires that students operate at relativistic levels. Students need techniques through which truth or falsehood, validity or invalidity is established. The Perry model can help the faculty to clarify the diversity of thinking that students bring to a topic. The model also suggests that many of the expectations for student understanding of sophisticated concepts are beyond many students' levels of cognitive development.

HOW STUDENTS BECOME ADULT LEARNERS

So far we have discussed the learning needs and expectations of 18- to 25-year-olds. This includes the expectation of finding the "truth" or the "right" answer. However, most of life's decisions are adaptive decisions, for example, decisions that require dealing with ambiguity and choosing from all of the options which are good or best for the decision maker. Certainly, these kinds of scenarios describe the modern workplace in which the college graduate finds himself or herself.

Most young people are not cognitively equipped to deal with these kinds of sophisticated cognitive processes. Their brains may not become completely developed until the age of 25 (Sylvester, 2002). Until then, emotional decision making is mostly used. Students have learned to resolve ambiguous situations by making decisions by trial and error.

Because the brain is a map-making or pattern-seeking organ, the way in which a student organizes new information—the degree to which he or she can create meaningful and familiar patterns—is the key to retaining the information. The information must be integrated into the student's permanent conceptual scheme. Helping students to discover the patterns that already exist in the content we teach helps them to become successful learners. Even more important is to connect new learning to old learning. The teaching tools that can help faculty connect to their students' backgrounds include the following:

- Analogy
- Metaphor
- Example (especially when the student's background is not specific to the new learning)

Because the average age of college students has trended upward in recent years, faculty need to be familiar with what Malcolm Knowles (1980) called *andragogy:* the art and science of helping adults to learn. Adults learn by five different methods: reading, hearing, seeing, saying, and doing. Research indicates that they absorb 10% of what is read, 20% of what is heard, 30% of what is read and heard, 50% of what is heard and seen, 70% of what is said by them, and 90% of what is done by them with others (NTL Institute, 1954). Simply stated, adults learn best by *doing*. This means they learn best by practicing skills and by using the skills to work on realistic problems. Also, they learn best when they are "ready" to learn, which means they see the importance and usefulness of the learning if the environment is adequate and comfortable. In addition, they learn best when material is presented in small amounts arranged in an organized way, when they have time to absorb it, and when they have a sense that they are making progress. It is interesting to note the differences between the characteristics of adult learners and those of the 18- to 25-year-olds.

Characteristics of Adult Learners

- Adults want to learn.
- Adults learn only what they feel a need to learn.
- Adults look to learn what can immediately be applied.
- Adults want to know if what they are asked to learn is relevant to their needs.
- Adults seek to learn what they have identified as important rather than what others deem important.
- Adults learn by doing.
- Adults are problem centered rather than subject centered.
- Adults have a broad base of experience on which to draw and share with others.
- Adults learn best in an informal environment.
- Adults learn best when a variety of methods are used in instruction.
- Adult learners tend to be less interested in survey courses.
- Adults want guidance, not grades.
- Adults' concepts about themselves directly affect their behavior and desire to learn.
- Adults have expectations, and it is critical to take time up front to clarify and articulate all expectations before getting into content.
- Adults learn best when programs are designed to accept viewpoints from people in different life stages and with different value "sets."

Most adult learners in the college classroom are managing a stressful life consisting of work, family, and school. In addition to this precarious work-life balance, adult learners often are dealing with psychological factors such as anxiety level and self-esteem, often over their skills with library and distance learning technologies. Adult learners will decide for themselves what is important to learn. However, their decision is deeply affected by the faculty's ability to explain that what is being taught is important.

The "Wh" of Teaching

- Where how does this current learning fit into future learning?
- Where how does this current learning fit into my career goals?
- Where (in what other classes) will I use these skills or information?
- What makes this learning important?

- Why do I need to learn this in this particular way?
- Why do we have to learn in groups?
- Why do I have to speak in public?
- Why do you make us do all the work?
- Why do you give cumulative exams?
- Why do I have to teach other students?
- Why do we have to write summaries?

Two principles of learning, the primacy and recency effects, are important for faculty to incorporate into their instructional methods. Information learned first creates a strong impression in the mind that is difficult to erase. Information that is presented in the first 20 minutes of class (primacy) will receive the students' great attention and present the best chance to be recalled in the future. Information presented in the last 10 minutes of class (recency) has the next best chance of being recalled (Sousa, 1991). The NTL Institute (see Table 3.1) showed that teaching others is the teaching method that has the most potential for retention, whereas lecture has the least potential. Perry (1981) suggested that lectures utilize content that weaves among emotional, social, and cognitive systems.

As noted earlier, information gets connected to prior knowledge when linkages in the brain create new pathways for the information to be recalled. For faculty, the point is that the relevance and importance of the information influences what the student retains (Zull, 2002). When the information or skills are

Table 3.1	Teaching Methods' Effect on Retention (NTL Institute)
Retention After 24 Hours	
Lecture	5%
Reading	10%
Audiovisual	20%
Demonstration	30%
Discussion Group	50%
Practice by Doing	75%
Teaching Others	90%

elaborated, for example, when the student tries to find additional connections to prior knowledge, retention is enhanced. One way faculty can encourage these additional "connections" is to have students put the information into their own words or "recode" it. Summary writing is a good example of making connections to already existing patterns in the brain. Other assignments might include having students teach each other, present their work in public, or engage in classroom discussions. Research also reinforces the value of homework. Students who do homework that reinforces learning and applies to information learned earn 25% gains in test results. If the homework is graded, the increase reaches 30% (Bransford, Brown, & Cocking, 1999; Marzano, Pickering, & Pollack, 2001).

Although there is disagreement among neuroscientists regarding the legitimacy of matching individual learning styles to complementary instruction, there is general agreement that students should do as much multisensory learning as possible (Conway, Gardiner, Perfect, Anderson, & Cohen, 1997). Multisensory learning methods include labs, internships, field trips, service learning, case studies, solving ill-structured problems, preparing test questions, and making presentations to authentic audiences.

REACHING AND RELATING TO STUDENTS

Traditionally, adjunct faculty have considered themselves to be subject matter experts, hired to teach a course in their area of specialty. In reality, to be effective in the classroom, the faculty should recognize that learning involves much more than the information conveyed. Learning is a social and emotional experience and faculty teach the whole person, not just the cognitive mind (Angelo, n.d.).

There are several ways to create a pleasurable learning environment. One way that all faculty can relate to is to get the students' attention. Attention is a cognitive process that allows a student to control irrelevant stimuli, notice important stimuli, and shift from one stimulus to another (Anderson & Krathwohl, 2001). A significant part of getting students to attend class is to use "novelty" in instructional methods, processes, content, or tools. For example, Dr. John Fry of Marymount University in Arlington, Virginia, dressed up as the television private investigator, Columbo, to demonstrate questioning techniques in his behavior modeling class.

Emotional arousal is also effective at creating and spreading pleasure, as long as it isn't the emotion of fear or anxiety. Effective faculty use music, journaling, storytelling, and debates as ways to arouse emotions and create effective learning conditions.

An advance organizer is another tool for focusing students' attention. These organizers use familiar terms and concepts to link what students already know to new information that will be presented in the lesson, which aids in the process of transforming knowledge and creatively applying it in new situations. This process helps to embed the new content in long-term memory. Advance organizers do not have to be long or complex, just clear and relevant to the material. Table 3.2 shows an example of an advance organizer.

Table 3.2	Agree/Disagree Chart
Agree	**Disagree**
The United States should have nationalized health care.	The United States should not have nationalized health care.

DIALOGUE IN THE CLASSROOM

One of the most powerful tools faculty have to encourage learning is dialogue. Skillful dialogue in the classroom involves the often painful process of developing and applying critical thinking to the learning conversations. What is critical thinking? Critical thinking is self-guided, self-disciplined thinking which attempts to reason at the highest level of quality in a fair-minded way. People who think critically consistently attempt to live rationally, reasonably, and empathically (see criticalthinking.org). Skillful dialogue consists of three skills: (a) Clarify your thinking, (b) inquire into others' thinking, and (c) test assumptions.

According to Elder and Paul (1996b), our muddled, deceptive, or misleading thinking often brings about significant problems in communication. The only way to correct this is to clarify our thinking by searching for and communicating the meaning in our words more clearly and specifically. Strategies for clarifying your thinking follow:

- State one point at a time.
- Elaborate on what you mean.
- Give examples that connect your thoughts to life experiences.

- Use analogies and metaphors to help people connect your ideas to a variety of things they already understand.

A format for teaching students (and yourself!) to clarify thinking follows.

Format for Clarifying Thinking

- I think . . . (state your point)
- In other words . . . (elaborate your main point)
- For example . . . (give an example of your main point)
- To give you an analogy . . . (give an illustration of your main point; see Elder & Paul, 1996b)

To inquire into and clarify others' thinking, Elder and Paul (1996b) proposed a set of powerful questions:

- Can you restate your point in other words? I didn't understand you.
- Can you give an example?
- Let me tell you what I understand you to be saying. Did I understand you correctly?

The intent of these questions is to not only engage the students in the learning discussion but to provoke them to examine their own thinking for a high standard of relevance, accuracy, specificity, and logic.

The third skill in dialogue is the ability to test your and others' assumptions. Be watchful for fuzzy or illogical thinking. Stay focused on what is relevant and what will aid you and the students in solving a problem. If a student offers an idea that doesn't seem pertinent, don't hesitate to ask, "How is what you are saying relevant to the issue?" Following is a list of other questions you can ask to encourage disciplined thinking and test assumptions:

- Have I focused on the main problem or task?
- Have I missed anything?
- Where do we need to focus our attention?
- Are we being diverted to unrelated matters?
- Am I failing to consider unrelated viewpoints?
- How is your viewpoint related to the issue we are addressing?

- What other facts would help us answer the question?
- What considerations should be set aside?
- How does this connect to the question?

QUESTIONING SKILLS

As we have seen, questions are significant to the learning process. Asking the right questions at the right time, in the right way, contributes to the learning of all. The following list provides types of questions and examples:

Overhead: Directed to the entire group to promote thinking. Example: "How will communication patterns change in the next decade?"

Leading: Used to suggest an answer to prompt analysis. Example: "How might supervisors benefit from learning this?"

Clarifying: Used to challenge old ideas, develop new thoughts, or check understanding. Example: "How would that work in today's environment?"

Redirected: Returning a question posed by a student to the same student or to another in the class. Example: "That's a good question, Robert. What would you do in your organization, Maya?"

Factual: Used to obtain specific information, sometimes for the purpose of getting discussions started. Example: "How many of you work in matrix organizations?"

Alternative: Requires a decision between options; sometimes used to evaluate the options. Example: "Are the best managers strict, easy, or neither?"

Personal experience: Prompts sharing of past critical incidents, adding concreteness to the discussion, and promoting ownership of the topic. Example: "What experiences have you had with ISO 11000, and how has it affected the functioning of your organization?"

When framing questions:

- Be brief.
- Cover a single point.
- Relate the question directly to the topic.
- Use words that have meaning to the class.

Questions may be *open* or *closed*:

- *Open* questions cannot be answered by a "yes" or "no" or other one-word answers. They stimulate students' involvement by encouraging discussion. They generally begin with the words *what, when, where, which, how, who,* or *why;* for example, "Why are teams playing such an important role in industry today?"
- *Closed* questions can be answered by a "yes" or "no" or a one-word answer. They discourage discussion and may be seen as leading the class to an opinion. Closed questions generally begin with the words *is (are, aren't, was, wasn't), has (have, haven't), do (did, didn't), can (could, couldn't), will (would, wouldn't, won't),* or *shall (should).*

When directing questions, choose whether you want to direct your question to the class or to an individual. When you want to provide wider involvement, avoid putting individuals on the spot, or stimulate thinking, direct questions to the class. When you want to recognize a special resource, build on a previous contribution, or increase involvement from particular individuals, direct questions to an individual.

In general,

- Allow sufficient time for responses.
- Restate or reword the question if class members appear confused.
- If no one responds, select an individual for responding.
- Encourage the class to question one another.

Effective faculty will focus both on the quality and quantity of student responses and student reflection. The average wait time for faculty after asking a question is .9 second. Extending this wait time to 3 seconds will significantly improve student responses and interaction. Students will begin to ask their own questions and improve the quality of their understanding. When faculty interject short pauses of 3 to 10 seconds in their discussions, they send a message that they want their students to think and respond. Reflection leads to new understanding. Students need to know that doing the advanced preparations faculty ask, such as homework or reviewing notes, activates the prefrontal cortex of the brain. This ensures better performance in learning new material. Questions such as "What else?" or "Can you tell me more?" also stimulate reflection and more dialogue. Brainstorming is an excellent dialogue activity. It lets students tell what they already know and provides the hook to hang new information on. As students get comfortable in the dialogue environment, they will learn how they best learn and remember. This will reinforce their attention and ongoing learning.

Teaching students how to think is not driven by answers but by questions. Questions express problems and present issues, but only when an answer generates a further question does thought and learning continue. Effective college faculty do not want their students to simply assert a point of view; they want their students to try to reason things out with evidence, logic, and good testable inferences. This is why students who have questions are really thinking and learning. It's possible to give students a test on any subject by just asking them to list all the questions they have about a subject, including all questions generated by their first list of questions (Elder & Paul, 1996b). Questions of *purpose* force students to define the task. Questions of *information* force them to look at sources of information as well as at the quality of the information. Questions of *interpretation* force students to follow out where their thinking is going. Questions of *point of view* force them to examine their other irrelevant points of view. Questions of *accuracy* force them to evaluate and test for truth and correctness, and questions of precision examine students' thinking for contradictions. Questions of *logic* force students to consider how they are putting the whole of their thought together to make sure it all adds up and makes sense within a reasonable system of some kind.

So, the fine art of questioning involves both teaching with carefully crafted questions and teaching students how to ask the right kinds of questions. The following list illustrates the fine art of probing through questions:

Questions to Facilitate a Book Discussion

- What is the purpose for the book?
- What is the author trying to accomplish?
- What issues or problems are raised?
- What data, what experiences, what evidence are given?
- What concepts are used to organize this data, these experiences?
- How is the author thinking about the world?
- Is the author's thinking justified as far as we can see from our perspective?
- And how does the author justify it from his or her perspective?
- How can we enter the author's perspective to appreciate what he or she has to say? (Elder & Paul, 1996b)

LEARNING STRATEGIES FOR THE ONLINE CLASSROOM

Many colleges and universities now offer both online and blended learning classrooms. The task of developing online instructional strategies and facilitating in the online learning environment is daunting for any faculty, much less the adjunct college faculty. Numerous authors have addressed this issue; however, several common elements appear in one form or another:

1. *Lesson Length:* Unlike lesson plans in face-to-face classroom, lessons in the online classroom should be in 15- to 30-minute chunks to accommodate log-in time. In general, there is a three-click rule in instructional design for the World Wide Web. Any piece of information should be viewable by no more than three clicks of the mouse on the browser's scroll bar on the screen.

2. *Taking the Lesson With Them:* Web pages should be printable so that students can take the information along when they are offline.

3. *The Effective Syllabus:* The online syllabus should also contain information relating to length of time a given assignment is anticipated to take for average students so they can schedule the activity into their available time.

4. *Make Suggestions:* The faculty should make suggestions to the students about how they can manage and make the best possible use of the time they devote to the course. These suggestions can include setting times for logon, creating a schedule for assignments, composing posts, and late messaging.

5. *Providing Clear Posting Requirements:* It is a good idea to give specific minimum and maximum requirements concerning number of posts students are required to submit so that they schedule time properly to meet expectations.

6. *Motivate Beyond the Grade:* Build interest and relevance into and throughout the course. Involve the students and build discovery whenever possible. Reward and encourage students. Frequently provide personal feedback via e-mail and student-specific forums. Respond promptly and effectively to student posts. Use the faculty's page effectively by giving an image of yourself. Ask for student feedback. Break the ice at the beginning of the course and be engaging, even funny when appropriate. To create and maintain the online community, foster effective communication among the students (Varvel, 2001).

Establishing an Environment for Learning

As college students shift toward adult learner demographics, their expectations of faculty shift from the traditional teaching role to one of facilitator of learning. Traditional teaching tends to be more didactic. In other words, teachers instruct and inform their students. Facilitators help a group of learners define its goals and objectives, assess its needs, and create plans to meet them. Facilitators provide and manage processes that help the group and individuals achieve their agreed-upon objectives. They create a positive environment in which learners can work productively to meet goals and they provide feedback so that the group and individuals can make adjustments. They put the learner first and trust the process to achieve results (Bens, 2005). Although college faculty will always need to know their subject, they will also need to manage and maintain a group process (see Appendix B: Checklist for Group Facilitation). It is important for the faculty to manage group activities to increase the learning of the students. Poor student interaction in group activities diminishes the students' confidence in the ability of the faculty.

Conclusion

In this chapter, we covered theories of student learning and students' readiness for learning. We talked about adult learning and how we need to change our instructional strategies and approaches for our growing numbers of adult learners, and we discussed what makes different students view the role of the teacher differently. The chapter also covered ways to reach out and relate to students by honing the adjunct faculty's questioning skills. We elaborated on the use of dialogue in the classroom to clarify thinking, both of the students and that of the adjunct faculty. We ended the chapter with a discussion about learning strategies for the online classroom and establishing an environment for learning.

References

Angelo, T. (n.d.). *Understanding how college students learn.* Retrieved July 15, 2009, from http://www.ferris.edu

Anderson, L., & Krathwohl, D. (Eds.). (2001). *A taxonomy for learning, teaching and assessing: A revision of Bloom's taxonomy of educational objectives: Complete edition.* New York: Longman.

Bens, I. (2005). *Facilitating with ease!* San Francisco: John Wiley & Sons.

Blumberg, M. (2004). Beginning journey toward a culture of learning centered teaching. *Journal of Student Centered Learning, 2*(1), 68–80.

Bransford, J., Brown A., & Cocking, R. (Eds.). (1999). *How people learn: Brain, mind, experience, and school.* Washington, DC: National Academy Press.

Conway, M. A., Gardiner, J. M., Perfect, T. J., Anderson, S. J, & Cohen, G. M. (1997). Changes in memory awareness during learning. *Journal of Experimental Psychology, 126,* 393–413.

Covington, M. V. (1992). *Making the grade: A self-worth perspective on motivation and school reform.* New York: Cambridge University Press.

Dweck, C. (2000). *Self-theories: Their role in motivation, personality, and development.* New York: Psychology Press.

Elder, L., & Paul, R. (1996a). *The critical mind is a questioning mind.* Retrieved August 13, 2009, from http://www.criticalthinking.org/articles/critical-mind.cfm

Elder, L., & Paul, R. (1996b). *Becoming a critic of your thinking.* Retrieved January 12, 2009, from http://www.criticalthinking.org/page.cfm?PageID=478&CategoryID=68

Knowles, M. S. (1980). *The modern practice of adult education: From pedagogy to andragogy* (Rev. ed.). Englewood Cliffs, NJ: Prentice Hall.

Marzano, R. J., Pickering, D. J., & Pollack, J. E. (2001). *Classroom instruction that works: Research-based strategies for increasing student achievement.* Alexandria, VA: Association for Supervision and Curriculum Development.

NTL Institute for Applied Behavioral Science. (1954). *The learning pyramid.* Retrieved August, 13, 2009, from http://siteresources.worldbank.org/DEVMARKET PLACE/Resources/Handout_TheLearningPyramid.pdf

Perry, W. Jr. (1970). *Forms of intellectual and ethical development in the college years: A scheme.* New York: Holt, Rinehart & Winston.

Perry, W. Jr. (1981). Cognitive and ethical growth: The making of meaning. In Arthur W. Chickering and Associates (Eds.), *The modern American college* (pp. 76–116). San Francisco: Jossey-Bass.

Sousa, D. (1991). *How the brain learns.* Thousand Oaks, CA: Corwin.

Steinberg, L. (1996). *Adolescence.* New York: McGraw-Hill.

Sylvester, R. (2002). *A celebration of neurons: An educator's guide to the human brain.* Alexandria, VA: Association for Supervision and Curriculum Development.

Varvel, V. Jr. (2001). *Facilitating every student in an online course.* Retrieved August 10, 2009, from http://www.ion.uillinois.edu/resources/pointersclickers/2001_03/index.asp

Weimer, M. (2002). *Learner-centered teaching.* San Francisco: Jossey-Bass.

Zull, J. (2002). *The art of changing the brain.* Sterling, VA: Stylus Publishing.

Teaching Methods

Preparation and Application

Cynthia H. Roman

Chapter 4 begins with emphasis on instructional strategies both teacher-centered and learner-centered. Learner-centered approaches to instruction involve the faculty member serving in the role of "facilitator" as students construct their own understandings. Here Cynthia Roman includes an expansive offering of teaching methods, many with Internet reference sites noted. A sample listing includes problem-based learning and inquiry, multimedia stories, collaborative learning, web-based forums, and learning contracts.

Most helpful to any adjunct faculty member, part- or full-time, are the chapter sections on evaluating learning, developing lesson plans, and creating the course syllabus. Of note in the second part of the chapter is the inclusion of a section on giving feedback, which requires two considerations for success: following a process and using effective techniques. Here Roman details a useful model that may also be adapted for use in a peer evaluation process along with offering tips for overcoming student objections or resistance to feedback.

Finally, Roman discusses the critical treatment of outcomes evaluation (criterion-referenced) where a student's level of achievement is measured against curriculum objectives and course goals. This concluding chapter section brings together an explanation of and focus on assessment as an empirical approach to making decisions about teaching and learning.

INSTRUCTIONAL STRATEGIES

An instructional method is an overall approach for facilitating learning. Examples of instructional methods are lecture, discussion, demonstration, reading assignment, and field trip. Within each method, various media can be used. Media are channels through which information is transmitted, for example, CD, video, and electronic slides.

Teacher-Centered Approaches

Teacher-centered approaches include instruction where the teacher's role is to present the information that is to be learned and to direct the learning process of students (Shuell, 1996). The teacher identifies the lesson objectives and takes the primary responsibility for guiding the instruction by explanation of the information and modeling. This is followed by student practice. Methods that fall into the teacher-centered approaches include demonstration, direct instruction, lecture, and lecture-discussions.

Demonstration involves the teacher showing students a process or procedure such a science process, a cooking procedure, or a computer procedure. Involving students in demonstrations allows this method to be less passive.

Direct instruction is used to help students learn concepts and skills. There are various models of direct instruction but all include similar steps: (a) introduction and review, (b) presentation of new information, (c) guided practice, and (d) independent practice.

Lecture is the most criticized of all teaching methods and the most commonly used because (a) planning time is limited, (b) lectures are flexible and can be applied to any content, and (c) lectures are simple. The most critical fact about lecture is that it puts students in a passive role. **Lecture-discussion** is a combination of lecture and teacher questioning of students.

Learner-Centered Approaches

Grounded in constructivism, learner-centered approaches involve instruction where the teacher is a facilitator as the learners construct their own understandings. There are a number of methods in this category that are listed and explained here.

Case studies involve groups of students working together to analyze a "case" that has been written on a particular situation or problem to find a solution. Case studies allow students to apply new knowledge and skills for solving complex issues. This method is not appropriate for use with elementary students. The case study is completed by discussion of the case, allowing learners to debate their conclusions. Case studies are discussed later under online instructional strategies.

Cooperative learning involves small heterogeneous student groups working together to solve a problem or complete a task. All students in the group must actively participate with each student while maintaining some independence. The success of the group depends on the input of each individual. The cooperative learning teaching method promotes the following:

- Active participation
- Individual accountability
- Students' ability to work cooperatively
- Improvement of social skills

Designed to encourage thinking skills, discussion allows learners to increase interpersonal skills. Discussions may occur in the classroom or online. One way to implement discussions with 21st-century students is to use discussion boards. Previously referred to as "bulletin boards" or "message boards," these areas are places where faculty can post a question and students may post "threads" (comments to the question) asynchronously (at various times). Discussion boards vary in participation, and good discussion may result from the expertise of the facilitator. Incentives (bonus points) may be needed to motivate all students and rules must be made clear. Learning management software (e.g., Blackboard) has built in a discussion board feature, making it quite easy to implement.

Discovery learning is an inquiry-based learning method in which learners use prior knowledge and experience to discover new information that they use to construct learning. This method is the most successful if the student has some prerequisite knowledge and the experience is structured (Roblyer, 1997).

Graphic organizers are found in the form of diagrams, maps, and webs and illustrate information in a graphical format. This strategy or tool can be used when brainstorming ideas, analyzing stories, analyzing characters, comparing and contrasting information, storyboarding (planning projects), prewriting during the writing process, and breaking down concepts to show the relationships with parts (such a the parts of a cell). These graphical representations of information have been found to make information easier to learn and understand, especially complex information (Dye, 2000). Further, using visual learning strategies have been found to be effective with struggling learners (Bulgren, Schumaker, & Deschler, 1988; Gardill & Jitendra, 1999, cited in O'Bannon & Puckett, 2007).

Journals are often used in classrooms to allow students to record reflections and ideas. Typically written in a notebook and recorded each day, the journal serves as a method of communication between the student and the teacher. A *blog* is short for web log and is simply an online journal or diary versus its more traditional "notebook" cousin. A new method for reflective writing, blogs can be used to share ideas and thoughts on various subjects. These reflections and ideas may be private or public. Blogs are considered great motivators for student writing and offer a novel way for students to engage in reflective writing and sharing information on classroom topics.

Know–What to Know–Learned is a strategy that is typically used to provide structure to the learning process to allow students to recall *what they know* about a topic, *what they want to know* about the topic, and *what is to be learned* (Ogle, 1986). This strategy allows students to become actively involved in their learning. Generally, a chart is created on the board, overhead, or handout. Students fill in the *Know* column before they begin their study and then fill in the *Want to Know* column with all of the information that they want to learn about the topic. After the study, they complete the *Learned* column with their new knowledge. An online generator of K-W-L charts can be found at teachnology.com/web_tools/graphic_org/kwl/

Learning centers are self-contained areas where students work independently or with small groups (pairs or triads) to complete a task. Learning centers may take the form of chairs placed around a table for group discussion; display boards that present questions, problems, or worksheets; computers where students perform hands-on activities; or research on the World Wide Web.

Role-play deals with solving problems through action. A problem is identified, acted out, and discussed. The role-play process provides students with an opportunity to (a) explore their feelings, (b) gain insight about their attitudes, and (c) increase problem-solving skills.

Scaffolding involves the teacher modeling the skill and thinking for the student. As the student increases understanding, the teacher withdraws the assistance, allowing the student to take on more responsibility for the learning.

Problem-based learning and inquiry involves the teacher giving the student a problem where inquiry must be utilized to solve the problem. There are commonly four steps in this model: (a) student receives the problem, (b) student gathers data, (c) student organizes data and attempts an explanation to the problem, and (d) students analyze the strategies they used to solve the problem.

A well-known and highly successful inquiry-based strategy is *WebQuests*, developed by Dr. Bernie Dodge at San Diego University (see webquest.org). This technique requires that answers to the problem in the quest be drawn from the World Wide Web.

Simulations are used to put the student in a "real" situation without taking the risks. Simulations are meant to be as realistic as possible, where students are able to experience consequences of their behavior and decisions. Simulations are commonly used in social studies and science but can be used in other curriculum areas. Computer simulations are quite common in today's virtual world. One example is "dissecting a frog" using the computer.

A great way to strengthen communication skills is to get students involved in creating **multimedia stories.** Topics can range from biographical stories with photo collections from family archives to community mapping projects, virtual field trips within the community, or more complex stories created by older students. These digital stories can be planned, storyboarded, and produced using slideshow software such as PowerPoint or video editing software such as iMovie. This strategy has become quite the rage in recent years, with students loving the active learning (see pbs.org/americanfamily/teacher3.html).

For the online learning environment, remember that you will want to create different ways in which the learner can master the content. Many of the following strategies are used in conjunction with other instructional strategies. For example, when you have students work in group projects, they are participating in collaborative learning, using small groups, and using a project instructional strategy. Following are some of the more common instructional methods you can use in an online or distance-delivered course.

Self-directed learning: Research shows that a student who initiates learning has more of a purpose and greater motivation. He or she also tends to retain and make better use of what is learned. Some activities you could suggest for students that take on self-directed learning projects are to visit libraries, institutes, and museums; talk to professionals; access recent research; and even create publications in a variety of formats. Some characteristics of self-directed learning follow:

- Learning is initiated and directed by the learner.
- The responsibility for learning is placed directly on the learner.
- Online learning supports pursuing individualized, self-paced learning activities.

Lectures can be presented via audio or video over the Internet and web-embedded online lectures. Some characteristics and features follow:

- Lectures allow the educator to lay the foundation for future student work.
- Lectures are most effective when used with other instructional strategies.
- Online lectures should be shorter and more to the point than traditional lectures.
- Lectures provides information to serve as a basis for further readings, research, and so forth.

Discussions are particularly effective with adults. Allowing adults to utilize their prior experiences is important. Some ways discussions can take place in a distance environment are with chats and bulletin boards. Some features of discussion follow:

- Listed as most favored by adults
- Interactive
- Encourages active, participatory learning

Small groups allow students to be highly involved with a concept or topic. This strategy allows students to present their ideas as well as get the ideas of others. The faculty's role in small groups is to act as a consultant to the groups. The faculty can address specific questions, comments, or concerns one group has while another group(s) can continue working. Some characteristics follow:

- Small groups give learners the opportunity to discuss content, share ideas, and solve problems.
- Small-group work often operates on high intellectual levels (analysis, synthesis, and evaluation levels).

The use of **mentoring** can be an effective instructional strategy because it allows the mentor to serve as a guide rather than a provider of knowledge. The mentor can introduce the learner to new situations, interpret unknown elements, and help point out critical areas of knowledge to enable the learner to function within the field. Two web sites that feature mentoring are the Electronic Emissary (emissary.wm.edu/) and International Telementor Program (telementor.org/). Some benefits of mentoring follow:

- It promotes learner development by drawing out and giving form to what the student already knows.
- Technology allows for frequent communication between mentor and student.

Projects allow students to have practical experience with a concept and give a sense of accomplishment. These projects can be individual or group and shared with the class, groups, or only the faculty. Examples of projects can be found at these web sites: The Great Paper Airplane Challenge (teams.lacoe.edu/documentation/projects/math/airplane.html) and Keys to Successful Projects (lrs.ed.uiuc.edu/guidelines/Rogers.html). Features of projects follow:

- They permit learners to engage in a variety of learning activities and delve into the content and context of a concept.
- They can serve as a framework that supports a multitude of instructional strategies.

Learning contracts might be an instructional method somewhat newer to you. In public school and higher education, learning contracts are used to ensure that the student and the faculty agree in writing exactly what needs to happen for something to be deemed a "successful" learning experience. With adults, have the learners write their ideal contract and then *negotiate* what the final contract will be. A learning contract helps the educator and the learner share the responsibility of learning. Contract learning can result in deeper involvement, on the part of the learner, in the activities with which they are involved. Contracts also provide increased accountability and a means for learners to receive feedback on their progress to accomplish the learning objectives.

Collaborative learning is simply working with others, and in the university coursework of today, collaborative learning is made easier through the use of technology. Although students might be separated by distance, they can use programs such as NetMeeting® to simultaneously work on documents, share files, chat, and more.

Case studies are becoming more and more popular. When evaluating case studies for use in your learning environment, you want to make sure sufficient detail is included so students can partake in powerful problem solving. The River Dammed: The Proposed Removal of the Lower Snake River Dams (see ublib.buffalo .edu/libraries/projects/cases/snake_river/snake_river.html) is an example of a case study. Case studies require learners to draw on their past experiences and use higher order thinking to "solve problems." It is extremely important to select an appropriate problem situation that is relevant to (a) student interests, (b) their experience levels, and (c) the concepts being taught.

Forums are also becoming more popular with the use of telecommunications. Synchronous and asynchronous tools, two-way audio-video, and other technologies allow forums to be used in distance education.

EVALUATING LEARNING

Current practice in evaluation is that college faculty spend many hours developing grading systems and then reviewing quizzes and exams, all in the quest for meaningful feedback. Most research does support that clear, specific, and timely feedback in which students are helped to find the right way to learn is more effective than feedback in which they are simply told whether they are right or wrong (Anderson, Corbett, Koedinger, & Pelletier, 1995; Anderson, & Krathwohl, 2001; McKendree, 1990; Sims-Knight & Upchurch, 2001). Also, helping students to learn how to assess and reflect on their state of learning will help them learn how to provide their own feedback and become independent, lifelong learners.

In designing a course, it is critical to have clear instructional goals and objectives. These goals and objectives should be stated in the course syllabus, along with the clear explanation of what is expected from the students, when it is expected, and why. Students should know, ideally before the beginning of the first class, what to expect, what will be required of them, what prerequisites are needed, and how their work will be graded.

Goals are broad statements on what you want to accomplish in your course and how your course will meet the learner's needs. Goals have been described as the "warm fuzzies" in the course-designing process, because although they sound desirable, how to achieve them is unclear (Mager, 1972). The goal addresses the general outcome, not the process. It does not refer to the specific activity in which the student will engage. For example, an art history course may have the goal of "broadening the student's appreciation of the Impressionist period," but the goal does not specify how this will be accomplished.

Objectives, on the other hand, support the goals of the course by indicating, in specific language, what the learner will actually do to achieve the goal(s) of the course. A good objective is a clear statement of what the student is expected to learn and what specifically will be measured to determine success. For example, in a course in introductory statistics, if the goal statement describes the aim of the course, it would be difficult to know, just from reading the goal statement by itself, what a student would need to do to achieve success in the course.

Thus, at some point before the course begins, the faculty needs to translate the goals into specific learner objectives. For example, in the introductory statistics course, one objective that supports the course goal could be, "Given a sample of data, the student will calculate the mean, mode, and standard deviation." In this case, the objective supports the goal of understanding nominal statistical measures and specifies a task that can be tested.

The process of writing objectives that are derived from goals is called *goal analysis.* Frequently this involves thinking about how people behave after they achieve the goal. Thus learning about these areas could become performance or learning objectives toward supporting the goal. It is from course objectives that more specific lesson plans and activities can be developed.

One way of performing a goal analysis is to follow a five-step process (Rothwell & Kazanas, 1992):

1. Identify, as clearly as possible, the goal that the instruction will achieve.

2. Write down examples of what people know, or do, when they have achieved the goal-identified behaviors associated with the goal.

3. Review the list. Eliminate duplications and objectives not clearly related to achieving the goal.

4. Describe in precise and measurable terms what learners need to do when they have achieved the goal.

5. Test the objectives. Can they be measured? Can they be tested through the test, class activities, or special assignments? Will the test or activity discriminate whether the student has successfully achieved the objective?

DEVELOPING LESSON PLANS

After the goals and objectives are determined for the course, you will need to develop individual lesson plans for each class meeting. Of course, you will not cover each goal and objective at every class meeting, so you will have to identify which objectives will be met during the class period. You will also have to decide on the most effective way to deliver the instruction. This means you need to think through what your students will expect and how they will best learn. Take into consideration whether your course is face-to-face or online.

You will need to determine which material students can best learn independently and which material requires a collaborative approach. You will need to decide which lessons can be passive (lectures, slides, videos) and which can be active (hands-on experimentation). Techniques can frequently be combined to make for a dynamic lesson filled with a variety of activities. The objectives should be driving which activities and assignments you select. For example, if you decide to show a video as part of the lesson plan, it should be because it supports a learning objective, not because it merely breaks up a boring lecture.

A lesson plan is a plan for student learning. Faculty who are new to teaching or who are teaching a course for the first time should develop complete lesson plans. Just as the syllabus represents the structure of the entire course, including the chronology, the lesson plan provides a structure for the individual class session. A lesson plan consists of an outline of the main topic(s) to be covered together with any subtopics associated with it, including the times and techniques devoted to each topic. The lesson plan should provide a review of the general and specific objectives you have set for the topic and the activities you have devised to ensure that the objectives are met. Having a detailed lesson plan gives the faculty an opportunity to revisit the lesson after the class is completed to determine what worked, what did not, and make notes for revision the next time the lesson is given. Appendix C contains a sample lesson plan that incorporates several different teaching methods and techniques.

COURSE SYLLABUS

All faculty members should provide students with a printed syllabus before, or at the latest by, the first class meeting. A course syllabus is a road map for the students, an aid to help them navigate through the course. It should contain the following:

- Course name, number, section, and location
- Date or semester
- Your name and home and office phone numbers and e-mail address, including best times to contact you
- Titles, authors, and editions of texts, required and recommended
- Course descriptions, goals, and objectives
- Tentative schedule of assignments and activities
- Testing, grading, and evaluation policies and procedures
- Attendance and participation policies
- Academic integrity policies

A good syllabus describes your balance among instructional strategies and your expectations for student involvement. As such, the syllabus reflects your educational philosophy as much as it is a navigational chart for your course.

Depending on college requirements, other types of information may be included. For example, the syllabus may include an honor code and violation information. Appendix D provides an example of a graduate syllabus.

GIVING STUDENTS FEEDBACK

Now that we have considered how goals and objectives are linked to your instructional and evaluation methods, you must consider the process of giving feedback, letting students know the results of your evaluation procedures.

An instructor gives students feedback in several ways. It is recommended that you use both written and verbal feedback techniques to maximize your effectiveness. Regardless of the mix of techniques, giving students feedback requires at least two key considerations for success: (a) following a process and (b) using effective techniques.

The following feedback process is a useful model to master. With little adaptation, the process can be used in peer evaluation processes as well:

1. Plan and prepare for giving feedback.
   - Adopt the attitude of a coach or facilitator of learning, not a judge.
   - Have a course and module goals and objectives available for easy reference.
   - Be ready to identify clearly accurate and acceptable knowledge and skills.

2. Ask the learner for a self-evaluation before you or others give feedback.
   - For significant feedback sessions, this should be done privately.

3. Make every effort to reduce student fear and anxiety.
   - Before your discussion, let the student know the date, time, and place for the feedback session.
   - At the start of the session, try to put the student at ease; give an overview of what will be covered and the benefits to the student.

4. Be candid, specific, direct, accurate, clear, and factual.
   - Give feedback on measurable and observable skills, not the individual. For example, it would not be appropriate to say, "You are so in love with your own voice that you did not provide the audience an opportunity to participate." A better way to give feedback about inadequate audience participation would be, "Your presentation did not allow

time for audience participation. In your next presentation, plan for at least 5 minutes of audience questioning. Keep your answers brief and to the point to encourage the maximum amount of audience participation."

5. Discuss how the student can improve knowledge and skills.
   • Involve the student in planning for improvement.
   • Set mutually acceptable, realistic goals for each student for a specified period of time that match the original course objectives.
   • Include checkpoints when you will reevaluate student progress in meeting the objectives.
   • Build on student strengths, rather than emphasize shortcomings.

6. Ask for the student's reaction to receiving the feedback.
   • Use effective listening techniques to get the full meaning of the student's attitudes, thoughts, and feelings.
   • Be sure that the student understands the feedback and buys into the plan for improvement. Ask for concurrence and commitment.

7. Take the opportunity to enhance your relationship with the student.
   • Help the student feel positive about objectives that have been accomplished and motivated to improve according to the agreed-on plan.
   • End on a positive note by emphasizing the success of the feedback session.

Throughout the process, you want to focus on techniques for making the feedback as effective as possible. Some of these techniques follow:

• Focus on specific knowledge and skills areas.
• Keep feedback impersonal.
• Tie feedback to the course objectives.
• Keep the time short between the evaluation and the receipt of the feedback.
• Direct constructive feedback at knowledge and behavior that the student can control.
• Ask the student to summarize the new behaviors that he or she will try in the future on the basis of the learning experience.

The last technique warrants a few more tips because overcoming student objections to feedback can be challenging. When you encounter student resistance, use the following process:

1. Acknowledge the student's emotional reaction to receiving feedback. Using a simple phrase such as, "I can understand that you must feel that way," can help the student move closer to accepting feedback.

2. Clarify the source and substance of the student's objection. Try not to jump to conclusions or make assumptions about what you think the student is saying. Use effective listening and paraphrasing to clarify the real source and substance of the objection. You can say, "So in other words, what you mean is . . ."

3. Confirm your understanding of the concern by rephrasing the objection in question form: for example, say, "Are you really concerned about . . . ?"

4. Respond to the objection directly. Indicate any student misconceptions, give relevant information, and offer proof to substantiate your explanations.

5. If necessary, reiterate your response in a different form. Consider using analogies or examples to clarify the issues in a new light for the student.

PROGRAM PHILOSOPHY

In general, the faculty must identify the philosophy, policy, and procedures regarding the subject of evaluation held by the program, department, school, and university. You can start this process by asking questions such as the following:

- What are the written and unwritten guidelines?
- Should I use norm-referenced methods or a criterion-referenced system?
- What is expected of me and of the students?
- Do most of the students work full-time? What effect does this have on student expectations of academic workload and on types and grading of academic assignments?
- Are there standards of evaluation?
- What effect does attendance have on evaluation?
- Are midterm and final exams required?
- Are there standard tests that I or someone must administer?
- What do my program head, department chair, dean, and president think about evaluation?

- What is the impact of grades on the students? What are their expectations?
- What do my tenured colleagues do? What are their thoughts about giving A's and about using the bell curve?

In short, the new faculty must scan the entire academic system to uncover written rules and unspoken assumptions concerning evaluation. The trend in evaluation is away from the norm-referenced methods of the past and toward the criterion-referenced (or outcomes evaluation) system more common today. The latter is based on curriculum objectives and course goals; grades depend on the student's level of achievement.

OUTCOMES ASSESSMENT

Assessment is an empirical approach to making decisions about teaching and learning. Good assessments are good research. Many new faculty feel that assigning grades is all they have to do to assess their students and their courses. Grades do assess overall proficiency but they do not provide detailed information about the specific strengths and weaknesses of a course. The value of outcomes assessment is that it answers the following questions:

- What should students be learning?
- In what ways should they be growing?
- What are students actually learning? In what ways are they actually growing?
- What should you be doing to facilitate student learning? How might you change assignments or instructional activities to improve actual student learning?

Assessments can be direct or indirect. Direct assessments require students to display their knowledge and skills as they respond to the instrument itself. Indirect assessments are surveys and interviews that ask students to reflect on their learning rather than to demonstrate it. Table 4.1 displays examples of both direct and indirect assessments.

Most universities provide formal end-of-course evaluations. In addition, the trend is to collect more outcome assessment data. These data will not only assist the faculty but they are increasingly being used to influence decisions about curriculum development, funding, and accreditation. You should ask your department administration about any responsibilities you have for collecting assessment data.

Table 4.1	Direct and Indirect Assessment Examples
Direct Assessments	**Indirect Assessments**
Examples:	Examples:
• All or a portion of students' term papers or lab reports	• Alumni or student surveys
• Objective tests, essays, presentations, and classroom assignments	• Employer surveys of satisfaction with student competence to perform the job
• Assignments based on capstone experiences (papers, portfolios)	• Exit interviews or focus groups (graduating students or alumni)
• Externally reviewed performances or exhibitions (musical, theatrical, dance, art exhibits, etc.)	• Interviews with instructors, residence hall leaders, and others who have contact with students
• Performance on state or national licensure, certification, or professional examinations	
• Standardized tests (nationally standardized or locally developed)	

CONCLUSION

We have shown how new adjunct faculty can benefit by adopting a learning-centered teaching approach. Our discussion has covered theories of student learning and what makes different students view the role of the teacher differently. We talked about adult learning and how we need to change our instructional strategies and approaches for our growing numbers of adult learners. We also discussed how to adapt instructional strategies for the online classroom. With so many tools in our toolbox, how can we miss? Finally, we addressed the growing importance of evaluation and assessment. The message is to come prepared to focus on the student and the learning process. It actually takes the pressure off you!

REFERENCES

Anderson, J., Corbett, A., Koedinger, K., & Pelletier, R. (1995). Cognitive tutors: Lessons learned. *The Journal of Learning Sciences, 4,* 167–207. Retrieved November 19, 2009, from http://act-r.psy.cmu.edu/papers/Lessons_Learned-abs.html

Anderson, L., & Krathwohl, D. (Eds.). (2001). *A taxonomy for learning, teaching and assessing: A revision of Bloom's taxonomy of educational objectives: Complete edition.* New York: Longman.

Atwater, L., & Brett, J. (2006). Feedback format: Does it influence managers' reactions to feedback? *Journal of Occupational and Organizational* Psychology, 79(4), 517–532.

Bulgren, J., Schumaker, J. B., & Deschler, D. (1988). Effectiveness of a concept teaching routine in enhancing the performance of LD students in secondary-level mainstream classes. *Learning Disability Quarterly, 11*(1), 3–17.

Dye, G. A. (2000). Graphic organizers to the rescue! Helping students link—and remember—information. *Teaching Exceptional Children, 32*(3), 72–76.

Gardill, M. C., & Jitendra, A. K. (1999). Advanced story map instruction: Effects on the reading comprehension of students with learning disabilities. *Journal of Special Education, 33*(1), 2–17.

Mager, R. (1972). *Goal analysis.* Belmont, CA: Pearson.

McKendree, J. (1990). Effective feedback content for tutoring complex skills. *Human-Computer Interaction, 5*(4), 381–413.

O'Bannon, B., & Puckett, K. (2007). *Preparing to use technology: A practical guide to curriculum integration.* Boston: Allyn & Bacon.

Ogle, D. (1986). K-W-L: A teaching model that develops active reading of expository text. *The Reading Teacher, 39,* 564–570.

Roblyer, M. (1997). *Integrating educational technology into teaching.* Upper Saddle River, NJ: Merrill/Prentice Hall.

Rothwell, W., & Kazanas, H. (1992). *Mastering the instructional design process.* San Francisco: Jossey-Bass.

Shuell, T. J. (1996). Teaching and learning in a classroom context. In D. C. Berliner & R. C. Calfee (Eds.), *Handbook of educational psychology* (pp. 726–764). New York: Macmillan.

Sims-Knight, J. E., & Upchurch, R. L. (2001). *What's wrong with giving students feedback?* Retrieved November 19, 2009, from http://www2.umassd.edu/cisw3/people/faculty/rupchurch/

Professional Development of the Adjunct Faculty

Jodi R. Cressman

Whether new or seasoned, all adjunct faculty share a fundamental development goal of discovering and using ways to assess and improve their teaching. Participation in formal and informal activities designed to enhance their teaching effectiveness and strengthen their students' learning is critical. As Jodi Cressman points out in Chapter 5, responsibility rests on both academic administrators and adjunct faculty to accomplish this aim.

Specifically for the adjunct faculty, in the first half of the chapter Cressman addresses a series of questions that answer how adjuncts may use evidence of learning to improve their teaching with specific examples of direct assessments, student self-assessment forms, student rating forms, and midterm feedback. Of particular note, she suggests exchanging teaching ideas with colleagues may be the best source for ideas on improving a course or adopting a new teaching method. Institutional and national higher education sources are also included.

The second half of the chapter shifts the focus and directs academic administrators such as department chairs, deans, program directors, or coordinators of adjunct faculty affairs to share institutional mission and values and expectations for learning along with available resources for developing teaching excellence. Encompassing suggestions that range from creating a course web site with sample syllabi, lesson plans, and assignments, to formal or informal mentoring programs that connect adjunct faculty to interested, experienced faculty, administrators are provided with useful professional development ideas that can be done with moderate time and cost. Cressman concludes the chapter with an encouraging reminder to include adjunct faculty in public recognition and rewards for innovation and excellence in teaching.

INTRODUCTION

Many of the chapters in this book cover topics that apply equally to adjunct and tenure-line faculty. After all, every college teacher needs to develop teaching and learning goals, employ appropriate teaching strategies, assess student learning, grade, and provide feedback to students. However, this chapter focuses on professional development, an area where adjunct and tenure-line faculty may have quite different needs, given that they typically have different responsibilities and roles within the university. For example, the most common and historically oldest form of professional development is the sabbatical, for which adjunct faculty are almost always ineligible (Sorcinelli, Austin, Eddy, & Beach, 2006). Other common professional development programs focus on career development (e.g., moving into the chair or other administrative roles, advancing a career post-tenure) or publishing research, which may not interest those adjunct faculty who think of teaching as supplementing (not constituting) their primary professions.

Despite these differences, all faculty, whether tenure-line or adjunct, new or experienced, share one fundamental faculty development need: finding ways to assess and improve their teaching. In pursuit of this goal, adjunct faculty should actively seek and have ready access to programs and activities that help them routinely reflect on strengths and challenges in their teaching, incorporate feedback from students and peers, and adapt their teaching methods and course design to strengthen their students' learning.

Many institutions have teaching centers dedicated to providing instructional support (consultations, videotaping, workshops), but there are many other professional development activities that can—and should—be done within an academic department, in collaboration with a colleague or on one's own.

Although this chapter has a single overarching aim—identifying ways for adjunct faculty to improve their teaching—it addresses itself to two different audiences. The first audience is the adjunct faculty himself or herself: How can faculty assess and strengthen their own teaching? How can they gather and reflect on evidence of their students' learning to identify areas of necessary improvement? How might they exchange teaching ideas, experiences, and innovations with their colleagues? And, finally, what institutional or national higher education resources might they draw on to strengthen their work?

The second part of this chapter is addressed to administrators (e.g., department chairs, deans, coordinators of adjunct faculty affairs). How can those responsible for recruiting, evaluating, and providing instructional development introduce adjunct faculty to their institution's mission, values, students, and expectations for learning? What relatively inexpensive resources can help adjunct faculty develop their own teaching?

PROFESSIONAL DEVELOPMENT ACTIVITIES FOR THE ADJUNCT FACULTY

Using Evidence of Learning to Improve Teaching

Direct assessments of learning: Frequent, focused classroom assessments are designed to expose weaknesses in student learning and thus identify points in your course where you may want to try new teaching methods or approaches. Every time you review student work or responses, ask yourself these questions: Did students achieve the learning goals? Were any of the results surprising or unexpected? What concepts or skills might require additional attention or new methods in teaching for the next class period or the next time you teach the course?

For example:

- At the end of a class period or course unit, ask students to take 1 minute to write on an index card or scrap paper the most significant thing they learned or a course concept that remains unclear or confusing to them. Review student responses before the next class period for patterns of misconceptions or ideas that you need to address before moving on to a new concept or course unit. Note: Although you are more likely to get accurate, candid information from students if you guarantee that you won't grade or even ask for their names on these kinds of assessments, it is important that students know that you read them carefully. Make sure that you begin the class after an informal assessment with a brief summary of the class response to the assessment question.
- Consider giving the students regular quizzes or short tests that focus on a single, complex concept so that you can monitor and quickly correct misconceptions before moving on in the course.

Are you looking for help? Staff at campus teaching centers, assessment offices, or even writing centers may be able to offer advice on administering frequent, low-stakes assessments of student learning. There are also a number of good online resources available. Start by visiting some of the web sites listed in Appendix E.

Student self-assessment forms: Consider asking your students to include with their major assignments a self-evaluation form in which they answer questions about their own effort in completing the assignment, their assessment of the extent to which their work achieved the learning goals, and the class activities they found to be most helpful in contributing to their success.

For example:

- Along with a paper assignment, give students a "self-evaluation" form in which they briefly connect the assignment to the course goals, describe the readings and/or course activities that contributed the most to their success in completing the assignment, and identify what they might do the next time they are asked to complete a similar paper. After reviewing student responses, note any changes you need to make the next time you teach the course. For example, do you need to revise the assignment so that students see its relevance to the course goals? Do you need to add to or adjust any activities that lead up to this big course project?
- For additional help in creating or interpreting these short self-assessment forms, consider visiting your campus teaching center or writing center.

Student ratings forms: Student evaluation forms provide summary data on teaching strengths and weaknesses. Although they often provide conflicting information (e.g., some students will single out as helpful the very same assignments and activities other students will suggest eliminating), they can indicate general areas to target improvement the next time you teach the course.

For example:

- If the evaluations point to a relative weakness in course organization, work on clarifying and sharing your course goals with students. Every assignment and course unit should be linked back to those overarching goals. You might also consider giving students a course "concept map" or even asking them to create one that shows how the ideas brought up in course readings and discussions are linked.
- If the evaluations suggest substantial student dissatisfaction with the fairness of grading, consider asking a fellow instructor to "grade" a small

batch of your student papers (with names removed). You might also review, revise (as appropriate), and disseminate your grading rubrics and/or criteria.

- If evaluations indicate that the material is too challenging, consider giving students more low-stakes opportunities to practice what they are learning; if students find the coursework too easy, ask students to complete more cognitively complex assignments (e.g., assignments that ask students to analyze and/or evaluate course concepts).

Midterm feedback: You don't need to wait until the term is over to gather input from students about what is working well and what needs improvement in the course. Ask students to take 15 minutes to complete an anonymous paper or online feedback forms.

Midterm survey questions might ask students what in the course is helping them learn, what you might do to help them learn more, and what they might do on their own to advance their own learning. New faculty are sometimes reluctant to gather midterm feedback, fearing that these surveys declare a weakness in teaching, but in reality, students already know (and may already be discussing among themselves) what is working and not working in the course. These surveys give the faculty member a chance to learn about and fix any miscommunications or major issues in a course while there is still time. Furthermore, in asking students to identify what they can do to learn more in the class, you are reinforcing the basic principle that although you are accountable for assessing and responding to your teaching, they are also accountable for their own learning. For examples of midterm surveys and questions, visit your campus teaching center or one of the online university teaching center pages listed in Appendix E.

Exchanging Teaching Ideas With Colleagues

The best resources for ideas on improving a course or adopting a new teaching method are likely to be your colleagues. Consider asking your department chair or administrator if you can participate in or even initiate the following:

- A listserv or e-mail conversation with other adjunct and/or full-time faculty
  - For example: An adjunct faculty teaching a historically challenging web site design course at a large private university e-mailed faculty who were currently teaching other course sections and asked them for their own

experiences in and strategies for teaching a particularly difficult concept. After a robust e-mail exchange, these instructors decided on their own to meet periodically so they could build a collective teaching "arsenal" of assignments that worked.

- The gathering and sharing of syllabi and/or assignments with other faculty

  ○ For example: Ask your department chair for sample syllabi and assignments to compare your learning objectives, assignments, and expectations with the department as a whole. Consider asking a tenure-line or veteran adjunct faculty to meet with you briefly to share his or her findings about what worked or didn't work when he or she last taught the course.

- The sharing and scoring of de-identified student work to compare expectations for student work

  ○ For example: Ask a colleague or two to report how they would score five of your student papers while you do the same for them.

- Small-Group Analysis (SGA)

  ○ For example: Like midterm surveys, SGAs allow you to identify and fix problem areas in a course before the term is over. They involve a peer instructor facilitating a class discussion (in your absence) in which students form a consensus around what elements in the course are effective in helping them learn and what concrete things you might do for the rest of the term to help them learn more. SGAs can be more helpful than midterm surveys because they offer the facilitator a chance to follow up with students and clarify their comments. For example, if a student volunteers that she doesn't like the group assignments, the facilitator can probe for additional details: What is it about them that is not helpful and how might they be revised or adapted so that they work better? SGAs may seem intimidating at first. After all, you are asking your students to discuss problems areas of your course with a colleague! But as long as you move to correct any substantial problems that surfaced in the process, your students are likely to appreciate your concern for their learning and value your dedication to improving your teaching. If your department doesn't have a formal SGA program set up, you might contact your campus teaching center or ask a trusted colleague to run the process in your class while you do the same for him or her.

Institutional and National Higher Education Resources

Many institutions offer teaching centers or offices of faculty development whose services typically include teaching consultations, workshops, seminars, classroom observations, and information about teaching conferences and events, many of which may come at no cost. However, even in those institutions without dedicated teaching or professional development centers, there are likely to be many expert professionals ready and willing to offer advice on particular areas of instruction. See the following, for example:

- In addition to helping faculty identify course materials, library staff members often have excellent suggestions for teaching research skills.
- Writing Center staff members have seen countless faculty writing assignments and may be willing to offer feedback on course assignments and suggestions for fast, effective grading.
- Although some assessment staff are more "on the ground" than others, they may be able to help you clarify learning outcomes or craft assessments that measure critical thinking or social responsibility or other typically complex, abstract learning goals.
- Instructional technology staff may agree to offer individual consultations or advice in addition to standard technology training.

You can also look beyond your institution to numerous teaching conferences and organizations devoted to improving college teaching. (See a selected list of teaching conferences and organizations in Appendix E.)

PROFESSIONAL DEVELOPMENT FOR ADJUNCT FACULTY: SUGGESTIONS FOR DEANS, CHAIRS, AND PROGRAM COORDINATORS

Given their limited financial and human resources, many departments and schools focus their professional development efforts on tenure-line faculty. However, providing useful information and feedback on teaching to all faculty, including adjuncts, can be done inexpensively and efficiently. For example, for little cost you can help adjunct faculty improve their teaching by doing the following:

- Share your department's learning outcomes and relevant assessment results with adjunct faculty. Adjunct faculty do more than teach a course: They contribute to students learning in the major curriculum. Help them understand and connect to the curriculum by sharing your overall learning goals for the major, asking them to explicitly link the course to the appropriate outcomes and adapt their course design to what your program assessments have demonstrated about areas of student strengths and weaknesses.

- Create a "course" web site with sample syllabi, assignments, rubrics, and best practices for teaching different classes. Use whatever course management system (e.g., Blackboard, Desire2Learn, etc.) is in place on your campus to create a shared space where adjunct faculty can readily access other instructors' course materials and post their own, ideally with annotations about what worked particularly well.
- Conduct an adjunct faculty orientation, conducted face-to-face or online. Strong orientations give faculty ample opportunity to meet other faculty (both tenure-line and adjunct), expose instructors to the department's learning goals and mission, and provide basic information about your department's students (e.g., how many of them go on to graduate school, how many commute or work over 25 hours a week, etc.).
- Provide a "commons" space (either physical or virtual) where new faculty can ask questions and share teaching ideas. If physical space and/or web support staff are limited, you might try using free social networking technologies (e.g., Facebook, Ning) to facilitate conversation and collaboration.
- Coordinate formal or informal mentoring programs connecting new adjunct faculty to experienced instructors. Good mentoring programs give new instructors ample low-risk opportunity to ask for advice and openly discuss teaching challenges. Encourage veteran faculty to mentor by acknowledging this work in annual reviews.
- Coordinate "brown bag" lunch meetings where faculty explore common teaching challenges.
- Provide recognition and rewards for adjunct faculty. Examples include dedicated teaching awards for adjunct faculty, programs that offer monetary rewards for participation in college or department faculty development events, dedicated grant funds for conference registration or travel and the creation of new course materials and/or new instructional technologies.

CONCLUSION

In keeping with the split focus of this chapter, I offer two different conclusions, one for adjunct faculty and one for the administrators that hire, evaluate, and support them.

For adjunct faculty: We expect our students to be honest in their self-appraisals and motivated to expand their knowledge and sharpen their skills. We should expect no less of ourselves as instructors. All teachers, regardless of status or role, can and should reflect on their teaching, revise their courses, and learn about and try new, effective teaching methods and tools. Happily, at many institutions, it is becoming a sign of teaching excellence rather than an admission of incompetence for all faculty (tenure-line and adjunct alike) to seek advice from local and national experts and to build and share collective knowledge about effective teaching practices.

For administrators: At too many institutions, professional development resources are devoted entirely to tenure-line faculty, leaving adjunct faculty with little other teaching feedback than what they glean from the typically scant, modestly helpful (at best) teaching evaluation forms. But faculty development should include adjunct faculty as well, especially because so much can be done with moderate time and cost. If you can do only a few things, focus on ways to connect adjunct faculty to the specific mission of your institution and department; give adjunct faculty ample opportunities (whether virtual or face-to-face) to exchange ideas, challenges, and information with one another; and find ways to publicly recognize innovation and excellence in teaching. Given that adjunct faculty may teach half (or more!) of undergraduate courses at many institutions, it is long past time to include them in faculty development efforts and support them in their reflections on and commitment to excellent teaching.

REFERENCE

Sorcinelli, M. D., Austin, A. E., Eddy, P. L., & Beach, A. L. (2006). *Creating the future of faculty development: Learning from the past, understanding the present.* Bolton, MA: Bolton.

6

Evaluation of Student Performance

Susanne Bruno Ninassi

Student evaluation—how, when, and why—is a challenging topic for new and continuing adjunct faculty. Departments or programs may require or suggest certain types of evaluations to be used in a course, yet oftentimes, the choice belongs to the adjunct faculty member. In Chapter 6, Susanne Ninassi details common methods or tools with clearly formulated criteria that adjunct faculty may use for evaluating students, including self- or peer evaluations. Samples of grading policies are provided along with an extended discussion of grading issues specifically highlighting point-value allocation and grading time management. This section of the chapter concludes with notes about dealing with student complaints and violations (or cheating), leading to the all-important next section: Academic Integrity.

Gone are the days of simply straining to see another's paper during an exam or preparing a tiny sheet of answers to be discreetly hidden in a shirt sleeve. Today's students have become extremely adept at using available technology in rather "creative" ways to take shortcuts. Ninassi's explanation of academic integrity as a fundamental value of teaching and learning, together with noted differences from university community misconduct policies and straightforward explanations of common violations of academic integrity (plagiarism, cheating, falsifying information, and facilitating academic dishonesty), provide every adjunct faculty—and any full-time professor—with a complete understanding.

Fundamentally, it is the responsibility of each adjunct faculty to create and maintain a climate of academic integrity in their courses and to support the institution's policies. This chapter concludes with details of preventive measures adjunct faculty may use, including the online service Turnitin and suggestions for policies governing the use of cell phones, iPods, and mp3 players in the classroom.

INTRODUCTION

This chapter describes the methods for evaluating student performance and the issues adjunct faculty face during this evaluation. This chapter also contains a discussion of violations of academic integrity and the impact of technology on academic integrity.

FACULTY EVALUATION OF STUDENTS

During the semester or term, the adjunct must assess and evaluate the student performance in the course. The purpose for evaluating student work is twofold. The first is to inform " . . . the instructor and students of the class's progress toward achieving the learning goals" and the second is to provide " . . . an opportunity for constructive feedback to further that progress" (Kaneb Center for Teaching & Learning, 2007a).

Methods used to assess and evaluate student performance are determined by the faculty member when planning the course and drafting the syllabus. The selection of the evaluation methods and the number of different methods used during the course will vary depending on the type of course and the subject matter. Also, the course objectives play a role in the selection of the method(s).

Each method utilized "should be based on clearly formulated criteria that are consonant with the learning goals for the course" (Kaneb Center for Teaching & Learning, 2007a). Once selected, the evaluation methods chosen must be communicated to the students, which will " . . . increase the reliability of the assessment and improve the student performance" (Kaneb Center for Teaching & Learning, 2007a).

The methods or tools for evaluation are numerous, but the common methods include the following:

- **Attendance**

Many faculty members require mandatory attendance, and students receive points if they attend all classes. However, points may be deducted for each missed class.

- **Class Participation**

The student's performance during class is assessed based on the student's response to questions, his or her participation in class discussions, as well as classroom interaction with other students. This method at times can be tied to attendance.

- **Examinations**

This method includes quizzes, tests, and examinations. Quizzes generally contain a few questions and can be spontaneous or scheduled. Quizzes are usually given to review a specific topic, to provide additional points, or to verify students' knowledge of the topic. Tests are scheduled and are designed to cover a particular topic, chapter, or chapters. Examinations can be synonymous with tests and cover multiple topics and/or chapters; however, exams are usually administered only once or twice a semester.

The types of questions used in quizzes, tests, or examinations include multiple choice, true or false, fill-in-the-blanks, short answers, essays, or any combination listed. In addition, quizzes, tests, and examinations can be closed-book, open-book, written, oral, or any combination.

- **Written Assignments**

These assignments can include more formalized writing assignments such as term papers, research papers, case studies, or briefs. Other written assignments can include letters, memorandums, or short homework assignments.

- **Oral Assignments**

Oral assignments can also include more formal presentations such as PowerPoint presentations or oral arguments. Other assignments include article review, recap of site visit (i.e., library, court, business), or informational presentation.

- **Team or Group Projects**

Team or group projects involve students working collaboratively on an assignment that can include either a written or oral presentation. The adjunct faculty evaluates the students' performance individually, as a group, or both. In addition, the adjunct faculty can request that the student conduct a self-evaluation, peer evaluation, or a combination of both.

SELF- AND PEER EVALUATIONS

Many of the methods previously listed can utilize self- and peer evaluations to evaluate student performance. Self- and peer evaluations are most commonly used in oral presentations and team or group projects. Upon completion of an assignment, the student completes a self-evaluation. This method can be completed simply as a brief written summary or by completion of a rubric or grading criteria.

For peer evaluation, students evaluate a student performance for a specific assignment or as a team or group member. As the student performs the assignment, each "peer" completes a rubric or grading criteria. The same rubric or grading criteria may be utilized for self- and peer evaluations.

GRADING POLICY

Once the determination of the types of methods to be utilized to evaluate the students is completed, the adjunct faculty assigns a point value to each assignment. This point system or grading policy is communicated to the student via the course syllabus or handout at the start of the course. This communication ensures that the students are fully aware of each requirement and the weight of each requirement, as each will affect the final grade.

Here are two examples of grading policies:

Example 1: Grading Policy (graduate level)

Requirement Point Value (out of 100%)

Class Participation	5
Writing Assignments:	
Research Paper	25
Case Brief	15

Midterm Examination	15
Final Examination	20
PowerPoint Presentation	20
Total points	100%

Example 2: Grading Policy (undergraduate level)

Requirement Point Value (out of 100%)

Class Participation	5
Homework Assignments (10)	10
Writing Assignment Term Paper (5–8 pages)	10
Quizzes	5
Tests (2)	10
Midterm Examination	20
Final Examination	20
Team Project (oral argument)	20
Total points	100%

Once the grading policy has been established, the adjunct faculty may be required to provide the numerical equivalent for grades as well as a grading policy. Colleges and universities identify the letter grades (i.e., A, B, C) to be used to evaluate students. Generally the adjunct faculty, with approval from the dean, determines the numerical equivalent for the grade. A sample follows:

93–100 =	A	77–79 =	C+
90–92 =	A-	73–76 =	C
87–89 =	B+	70–72 =	C-
83–86 =	B	60–69 =	D
80–82 =	B-	59–below =	F

GRADING ISSUES

The five issues discussed in this section are as follows:

1. Point value allocation

2. Time management

3. Consistency in grading

4. Student complaints

5. Violations

Point Value Allocation

How does an adjunct faculty allocate the point value and create the grading policy? As illustrated in Examples 1 and 2, each assignment is allotted a point value. The determination of the value is based on many factors, which include (but are not limited to) the type of course, subject matter, class objectives, and number of assignments utilized.

The assignments are "weighted" according to these factors as well as to their importance in the course. For example, in a quantitative course, a writing assignment may carry little weight; however, creating an Excel spreadsheet would receive a higher point value.

In Example 1, shown earlier, the research paper has a 25% point value in the course. It carries the most "weight" in respect to the remaining assignments. However, in Example 2, the value of the term paper is only 10% of the overall grade. The research paper in Example 1 requires higher levels of learning (analysis and synthesis). However, the term paper at the undergraduate level may require only comprehension and application.

Grading: Time Management

Once the course begins, the adjunct faculty starts evaluating student performance. As indicated earlier in this chapter, evaluation of student performance lets students know how the class is progressing and provides an opportunity for constructive feedback (Kaneb Center for Teaching & Learning, 2007a). "Instructor feedback guides the learning process and promotes student achievement" (Kaneb Center for Teaching & Learning, 2007b).

However, performance evaluation can be time consuming and at many times overwhelming. With multiple class loads, work schedules, and other obligations, adjunct faculty may have difficulty finding the time to review, grade, and record assignments. To eliminate some of the stress of grading, the adjunct faculty should utilize grading tools such as answer sheets or rubrics when designing an assignment. Use of these tools will help reduce grading time. Also, at the start of the course, the adjunct faculty may want to utilize Excel spreadsheets or Blackboard to record grades. These tools can be personalized for each course to calculate the point value as listed in the grading policy.

Assignments should be graded as soon as received. This is beneficial for the students (provides immediate feedback) and for the adjunct faculty (eliminates a "build up" of assignments to be graded). Also, at the start of a semester or term, adjunct faculty need to ask when the grades are due to the school and then plan accordingly. At the end of a semester, there is usually a very short window of time allotted from end of final exams to when final grades are due. The more prepared adjunct faculty can be, the less stress experienced meeting the deadlines.

As indicated earlier, the assignments should be graded immediately. Finding the time or managing time to complete this responsibility can be frustrating to adjunct faculty. To assist with this challenge and hopefully alleviate frustration, during the planning stages of their course, adjunct faculty should give consideration to the type of course, the number(s) of students, and the type of assignments to be given. If the instructor plans accordingly, especially when teaching multiple courses, he or she may be able to alleviate some of the time management issues.

For example, in a capstone class of 20 students, the final grade may be based on one end-of-semester presentation. The presentations are completed during the last week of class and at that time, the students are graded. Therefore, time management is not an issue because the grading is completed during class time. The only task left for the instructor is to record the grades. However, in a required introductory course, the instructor may have multiple sections totaling 60 students and he or she decides to assign five tests during the semester. The last test is given during finals week. The instructor may decide that the final test should be a mix of multiple choice, true or false, and fill-in-blanks questions as opposed to short answers and essays. It is less time consuming to grade a multiple choice, true or false, and fill-in-blanks test as opposed to an essay test.

The instructor should consider the length of time needed to grade an assignment as another means to assist with time management of grading. In a smaller size class, for example 12 students, grading an assignment or test may take 10 minutes per student; therefore 2 hours are required for grading. If the class size is larger, the time increases accordingly. If instructors know the length of time to grade an assignment, they can plan their schedules, which helps eliminate time management issues.

Consistency in Grading

When evaluating student performance, it is imperative that the grading be consistent. Issues arise when students believe individual grades were not consistent with others students' grades. One solution is to evaluate an assignment via the use of a rubric or grading criteria, which are reviewed and distributed with students at the start of the assignment. Not only does this ensure communication of the assignment requirements to the students, but it prevents inconsistent or partial grading by the adjunct faculty.

Student Complaints

Students may disagree with the grade received on an assignment. Although schools and universities may handle complaints in a specified procedure, generally, the student complaint should first be addressed to the adjunct faculty. The adjunct faculty and the student should meet to discuss the student's concern. The adjunct faculty can then review the assignment and the expected result via the textbook, class material, or rubric. If, after this meeting, the student still has a complaint, the student may seek counsel from an advisor or bring the complaint to the director or department chair. The director or department chair should notify the adjunct faculty of the contact and arrange to meet with the student, the adjunct faculty, or both.

Violations

During the evaluation process, an adjunct faculty may discover that a student has cheated or been dishonest on an assignment. This misconduct is an academic integrity violation. Most colleges or universities have an academic policy that all students are expected to follow. However, should a violation occur, adjunct faculty are expected to report the violation. The next section discusses in detail academic integrity and the types of academic integrity violations.

The Center for Academic Integrity (CAI), which is affiliated with the Robert J. Rutland Institute for Ethics at Clemson University in South Carolina, defines academic integrity

> ... as a commitment, even in the face of adversity, to five fundamental values: honesty, trust, fairness, respect, and responsibility. From these values flow principles of behavior that enable academic communities to translate ideals to action. (Center for Academic Integrity, 1999a)

Academic integrity is based on truthfulness of the students. Colleges and universities expect students "to foster in their own work the spirit of academic honesty and not to tolerate its abuse by others" (Center for Academic Integrity, 1999a). Academic integrity " . . . is a fundamental value of teaching, learning and scholarship" (Center for Academic Integrity, 1999b). Simply stated, learning institutions expect academic honesty and responsibility from each student. Violations of the academic integrity policy result in academic misconduct or academic dishonesty.

Difference Between Academic Integrity and Community Misconduct Policies

An academic integrity policy defines academic integrity, details the academic dishonesty or misconduct that constitutes an academic integrity violation, and lists the corresponding sanction should the student be found guilty. Also contained in an academic integrity policy are procedures for the reporting violations, the decision-making, and the appeals processes.

In addition to a policy on academic integrity, many institutions establish a code of conduct for the students. A code is a set of rules or regulations that detail the acceptable behavior and responsibilities of the students during their career at the institution. The purpose of the code of conduct is to ensure that the students have a safe and secure learning environment free from distraction, intimidation, physical or emotional harm, or violations to personal belongings and property (Marymount University, 2008–2009). The code of conduct policy explains the actions that constitute misconduct and lists the corresponding sanction should the student be found guilty. Also contained are procedures for reporting violations, decision-making, and appeals processes.

Many universities and schools will establish an academic integrity committee, which includes members of the faculty as well as student representatives. The purpose of this committee is to review the academic integrity policies and practices and to inform the faculty and students about policy changes. Also, committee members serve as panel members at academic integrity violation hearings.

Colleges and universities publish their academic policies on their web site, in student handbooks, and in other internal publications.

TYPES OF VIOLATIONS

The four common violations of academic integrity are plagiarism, cheating, falsifying information, and facilitating academic dishonesty.

Plagiarism

The Merriam Webster Online Dictionary defines *plagiarize* as "to steal and pass off (the ideas or words of another) as one's own; to use (another's production) without crediting the source; to commit literary theft; to present as new and original an idea or product derived from an existing source" (Merriam-Webster, n.d.). Wikipedia's definition of *plagiarism*, as part of academic dishonesty or misconduct, is "the adoption or reproduction of ideas or words or statements of another person without due acknowledgment" (Wikipedia, n.d.).

Plagiarism occurs when a student fails to acknowledge that the work submitted is not that of the student but of another. Although many institutions consider plagiarism as a form of cheating, it may be listed as a separate violation of academic integrity. Examples of plagiarism are varied but include failure to cite or properly cite another's work or purchasing or submitting a document from another (i.e., another student or an Internet source) and submitting it as one's own.

Cheating

Wikipedia's definition of *cheating* as part of academic dishonesty or misconduct is "any attempt to give or obtain assistance in a formal academic exercise (like an examination) without due acknowledgment" (Wikipedia, n.d.). In a current academic integrity policy, a description of cheating follows:

Cheating includes but is not limited to unauthorized copying from the work of another student, using notes or other unauthorized materials during an examination, giving or receiving information or assistance on work when it is expected that a student will do his/her own work, or engaging in any similar act that violates the concept of academic integrity. Cheating may occur on an examination, test, quiz, laboratory work report, theme, out of class assignment, during online work, or on any other work submitted by a student to fulfill course requirements and presented as solely the work of the student. (Marymount University, 2008)

Falsifying Information

Falsifying information in an academic setting occurs when a student submits information that is different (untrue) than what actually happened. Examples of this type of violation include providing untrue excuses for class absences or submitting a falsified document indicating a student completed all requirements for an internship.

Facilitating Academic Dishonesty

Under this violation, at least two or more students are involved. The violation occurs when a student asks others to perform the academic misconduct, and the other student(s) attempt or commit the misconduct. All students involved are charged with a violation because one benefited and the others participated. An example of this violation occurs if a student asks another to supply a copy of an exam or test.

ADJUNCT FACULTY'S ROLE

Unfortunately, according to recent research, part-time faculty members believe that enforcing integrity standards is not part of their job responsibilities (Hudd, Apgar, Bronson, & Lee, 2009). The part-time faculty members " . . . do not recognize the need for preventive strategies" (Hudd et al., 2009, p. 166). In addition, part-time faculty " . . . are less likely to take an active role in preventing integrity violations in their classrooms . . . are less likely to reduce the student's grade and they educate students less often about integrity concerns" (Hudd et al., 2009, p. 166).

However, "[p]art-time instructors play an important role in creating and maintaining a climate of integrity on campus. And so, their ideas must be used to inform academic integrity policies as they are developed and enforced" (Hudd et al., 2009, p. 164).

What Can Adjunct Faculty Do to Help Promote Academic Integrity?

The adjunct faculty should discuss academic integrity and the institution's policy with the students at the start of the course. Include in the syllabus the expectation of academic integrity and list the sanctions if a student commits a violation.

The adjunct faculty should monitor student's behavior in the classroom. As they are likely to be in the classroom during tests, they can "roam the room" and watch for signs of cheating and dishonesty. If academic conduct is discovered, the adjunct faculty should report the violation and impose a sanction.

ROLE OF TECHNOLOGY IN ACADEMIC INTEGRITY

The use of technology in the classroom has grown at an amazing rate. The Internet, for example, has opened a door for students to conduct academic research without leaving home. The Internet has also aided in combating academic violations. One tool utilized by colleges and universities is Turnitin.

Turnitin

In 1996, iParadigms, LLC created Turnitin.com, an online service that provides originality checking and plagiarism prevention. High schools and colleges utilize this service, which allows the schools to "check students' papers for originality against 75+ million student papers that have been previously submitted to Turnitin, and compares them to over 11 billion pages of web content including more than 10,000 subscription based journals and periodicals" (Turnitin, n.d.).

Turnitin uses document source analysis technology, which " . . . creates unique digital 'fingerprints' of each text document . . . and [t]hese 'fingerprints' are compared to others in the company's databases." This comparison . . . "ensures that papers can never be sold, recycled, or traded among students from different years, in other classes or at other institutions" (Turnitin, n.d.). The results of the comparisons are compiled into a report, which is available almost immediately to the adjunct faculty (Turnitin, n.d.).

The benefits of Turnitin are that the service is easy to use, database comparisons are huge (over 11 billion pages), and the comparison report is generated quickly. However, Turnitin "... *does not detect or determine plagiarism*" (Turnitin, n.d., emphasis in original). The service identifies text that is properly cited. The company recommends that "... instructors carefully review the Originality Report and all matches before making any determination of plagiarism. Such determinations of plagiarism require human judgment, and instructors and students alike should understand their institution's academic integrity policies before turning in written assignments" (Turnitin, n.d.).

Cell Phones, iPods, MP3 Players

Growth in technology has many positive impacts on the academic community. Unfortunately, this growth has lead to additional methods for students to commit academic integrity violations. Students use cell phones and text messaging, iPods, and other mp3 players to cheat during classroom activities as well as tests. These devices can be utilized in various ways. Cell phones can be used in a variety of ways during exams, not only to text another student for the answers, but to view photographed notes or other study materials that were taken prior to the exam. Many iPods and other mp3 players have Internet access capability; therefore, students can access the Internet for assistance during exams. In addition, students can use these devices to store data inputted prior to the exam, and during the exam or activity the student access these data.

Many faculty members restrict the use of these devices in their classrooms. This restriction may result in a reduction in the number of violations, but due to the size of some classes, students are still able to "sneak" and use the device undetected.

Writing Services

There are many writing services available to students via the Internet. For a fee, these services provide a custom paper written by a "professional writer" based on the specifications provided by the students (Barlett, 2009). The papers written by these writers are different from papers purchased by students from online databases. These papers "... are invisible to plagiarism-detection software" (Barlett, 2009).

Submitting a purchased paper from one of the services is plagiarism. However, because the papers are written new and are not papers recycled by students or databases, these papers go undetected by software such as Turnitin. Many schools have made efforts to close these mills, and a few states, including Virginia, have made selling college papers illegal (Barlett, 2009).

Researchers recommend that if the instructor suspects a purchased paper, the instructor should meet with students, discuss the paper, and should the student " . . . respond with blank stares and shrugged shoulders, there's a chance they haven't read, much less written, their own paper" (Barlett, 2009, para. 48). In addition, to combat the use of these papers, instructors may assign papers (i.e., reflective papers) that must be completed solely by the student (Barlett, 2009). It is important students learn what college is about and why studying actually matters to their future and the responsibility they must take concerning this learning. In addition, research by the Center for Academic Integrity shows "effective honor codes" and academic integrity policies can " . . . make a significant difference in student behaviors, attitudes and beliefs" (Center for Academic Integrity, 1999a, p. 2).

CONCLUSION

As an adjunct faculty, it is necessary to assess and evaluate the student performance in a course during the semester or term. Various evaluation methods as well as the issues surrounding performance evaluation have been discussed. In utilizing these methods and avoiding the issues, it is important for the instructor to plan and prepare for the course prior to the start of the semester or term. This preparation includes not only the completion of a syllabus, but also class lesson plans, assignment details and handouts, along with grading criteria rubrics for each assignment. Students will benefit from clearly communicated course demands and faculty expectations; adjunct faculty will benefit from time management.

Unfortunately, evaluation of student performance may lead to a discovery of an academic violation. As an adjunct faculty, it is necessary to be active in demanding and enforcing academic integrity. Preparation may also be one key to lessening academic dishonesty. Prior to the start of the semester, preparation may include obtaining and reviewing a copy of the school's academic integrity policy; structuring the course to include time to discuss the policy with the students, as well as sanctions (yours and the school's) for academic integrity violations; and discussing what activities constitute cheating or plagiarism in your class. Finally, before the start of a semester or term, determine what your policy will be regarding the use of electronic devices in your classroom. Be sure to include this policy in your syllabus and review it with the students. These measures should help deter and possibly eliminate academic dishonesty.

REFERENCES

Barlett, T. (2009, March 20). Cheating goes global as essay mills multiply. *The Chronicle of Higher Education, 44*(28). Retrieved July 29, 2009, from http://chronicle.com/free/v55/i28/28a00102.htm

Center for Academic Integrity. (1999a, October). *The fundamental values of academic integrity.* Retrieved July 29, 2009, from http://www.academicintegrity.org/fundamental_values_project/index.php

Center for Academic Integrity. (1999b, October). *Assessment guide.* Retrieved July 29, 2009, from http://www.academicintegrity.org/assessment_guide/index.php

Hudd, S., Apgar, C., Bronson, E., & Lee, R. (2009). Creating a campus culture of integrity: Comparing the perspectives of full- and part-time faculty. *The Journal of Higher Education, 80*(2), 146–177.

Kaneb Center for Teaching & Learning. (2007a, August 29). *Evaluation strategies.* Retrieved July 29, 2009, from http://kaneb.nd.edu/evidence/evaluation_strategies.html

Kaneb Center for Teaching & Learning. (2007b, August 29). *Examples of student work.* Retrieved July 29, 2009, from http://kaneb.nd.edu/evidence/student_work.html

Marymount University. (2008, October 1). *Academic integrity policy.* Retrieved July 29, 2009, from http://www.marymount.edu/academic/academic_integrity_policy.pdf

Marymount University. (2008–2009). *Student handbook.* Retrieved July 29, 2009 from http://www.marymount.edu/studentlife/studenthandbook/index.html

Merriam-Webster. (n.d.). Retrieved October 24, 2009, from http://www.merriam-webster.com/dictionary/plagiarize

Turnitin. (n.d.). Retrieved January 18, 2010, from http://turnitin.com/static/company.html

Wikipedia. (n.d.). Retrieved November 24, 2009, from http://en.wikipedia.org/wiki/Academic_dishonesty

7

Future Trends

Network Technologies and Adjunct Faculty

Terry D. Anderson, Vera L. B. Dolan, and Bryan A. Booth

This concluding chapter provides one of the most leading-edge ideas in the book: the capabilities of current and rapidly developing technologies to help adjunct faculty increase not only their professional competencies but also their academic networks.

Throughout the chapter, Terry Anderson, Vera Dolan, and Bryan Booth discuss network technologies and the impact on communication. This includes the effects on adjunct faculty's isolation or connection to the school and academic colleagues, professional development, instructional performance, and social networking to the larger academic community.

Anderson, Dolan, and Booth discuss the increase in virtual interactions and how they have provided a myriad of opportunities (and challenges) to adjunct faculty in performing their job. The sense of isolation, often felt by adjunct faculty that work from home offices or other distributed sites, creates challenges for these adjunct faculty as well as the hiring school. The authors provide suggestions on how to go beyond the technology training necessary to work in a virtual world, to methods to engage and include faculty into the larger community of the school. The blending of online, face-to-face, synchronous, and asynchronous communication, as well as the use of storytelling, connects the adjunct faculty to the school and improves the overall adjunct experience.

Using a model developed by Dron and Anderson (Taxonomy of the Many), the authors advance social networking contexts and their associated technologies, applications, learning designs, and outcomes. Beginning with groups, the authors discuss the extensive use of learning management systems (LMS), Web 2.0 group tools, and open source technology that are increasingly available to the adjunct faculty. Effective social networks (e.g., Facebook and LinkedIn), when properly used and integrated into the adjunct faculty's work, provide access to better teaching tools and practices, and they provide a means for the adjunct faculty to stay current in the field. Involvement in communities allows the adjunct faculty a productive connection to an aggregate of information (e.g., Cite-U-Like), which provides additional information and improves an *adjunct's* source of academic knowledge.

The primary application of the Taxonomy of the Many is the means to understand and provide adjunct faculty with the Internet tools to increase productivity, efficiency, and effectiveness. Increasing understanding and use of networking technologies provides adjunct faculty with many opportunities to market their skills, enhance their reputation, and increase social capital. Staying in touch with their profession allows adjunct faculty to be more valuable as faculty in their respective professional field.

INTRODUCTION

The capacity to communicate and network effectively is the basis on which competence, commitment, and presence are built and maintained in the lives of all professionals, including adjunct faculty. In this chapter we look at the many ways, both online and face-to-face, by which adjunct faculty can develop and grow their communication and networking skills. By becoming skillful communicators, adjunct faculty can reduce the sense of isolation or disconnectedness experienced by many distributed workers. As they become expert networkers and communicators, adjunct faculty are better able to perform their teaching duties and increase their enjoyment in work by achieving a greater connection to their students, their colleagues, and their school.

TECHNOLOGY-BASED COMMUNICATION AND IMPLICATIONS FOR ADJUNCT FACULTY

Sensing Isolation or Disconnectedness

Internet and web technologies have developed as an integral component of the learning environments in which most adjunct faculty now find themselves teaching. Given the pervasive effect of the Internet on communication, business, entertainment, travel, and education, it is not surprising that these new technologies, tools, practices, and cultural norms have significantly changed the nature of adjunct work. Moreover, it is unlikely that higher education has seen the end of this period of rapid change; technological advances will continue to shape adjunct faculty's work experience for the foreseeable future.

With this growth in virtual interactions, a sense of disconnectedness may also become evident among online instructors. A recent study investigated feelings of isolation among online adjunct faculty and examined how they coped with not having the same immediate access to peers, school staff, and management that characterizes traditional bricks-and-mortar environments, where workers can typically interact with others in nearby offices or within a relatively compact campus. For some adjunct faculty, the most negative aspect of isolation was the fact that they could not easily discuss academic issues with colleagues whenever they felt the need; others found the social isolation disturbing at times, given that most of the adjunct faculty studied were working from home and had no opportunities for face-to-face interaction with other faculty members (Dolan, 2009).

For a remote faculty member, the perception of being disconnected from academic issues and policies is not uncommon (Brindley, Zawacki, & Roberts, 2003). Adjunct faculty typically miss formal and informal interactions that are available only to those with physical proximity to colleagues and administrators. The sense of physical and psychological distance from management and coworkers may diminish an individual's sense of belonging, which can affect his or her motivation on the job.

Helping Faculty Feel More Connected

Administrators of institutions offering online courses are increasingly aware of the potential alienation that physical distance can cause to both administrators and faculty and are looking for ways to create a greater sense of community among online adjunct faculty. The principal rationale behind these attempts to strengthen community is the hope that online faculty will inform each other of critical institutional and discipline issues and exchange best practices, thereby improving their skills and sense of self-gratification. This in turn will enable schools to educate more effectively and retain students by providing superior services from more motivated faculty members.

An investment in professional development also increases faculty's sense of commitment (Gordon, 2003). At a time when the competition for students has become fierce, it is vitally important for administrators to extend the best possible treatment to adjunct faculty. Providing the means for these instructors to feel well supported, and consequently committed to quality in the delivery of their courses, allows schools to reap the benefits of attracting and retaining more students.

Unfortunately, adjunct faculty are not often provided with the necessary tools, training, or support to make full and effective use of currently available technology. If they are unable to count on support from the institutions for which they teach, they must make a substantial effort on their own to become more resourceful in acquiring and staying current with the tools and skills of their profession. Indeed, adjunct faculty must handle technology well in order to serve their students or face obsolescence (Camblin & Steger, 2000). Professional development activities coupled with individual exploration allow adjunct faculty to acquire the instructional and technological knowledge and skills required to be effective teachers (Eib & Miller, 2006).

Supporting Faculty—More Than Tech Training

Institutions have begun to focus on strengthening the faculty community so that instructors can exchange best practices and ultimately better serve students' needs. However, many have forgotten to take into account a basic intrinsic motivator: the need simply to socialize with others. In their quest to deliver quality education, many institutions are still struggling to define strategies for creating trust and loyalty in their adjunct faculty. Isolation resulting from physical distance seems to be a huge obstacle for nurturing meaningful, rewarding, and more personalized relationships. Feelings of disconnection from issues and policies affecting students, and from the overall organizational culture, impede efforts in training and development, as well as in coaching.

Many academic administrators, like their corporate counterparts who manage remote employees, may feel that providing access to a state-of-the-art virtual meeting space should be enough to create a sense of camaraderie and trust among online faculty. They may hope that high-end technology combined with a clear invitation for faculty to participate in discussions will create dialogue, knowledge exchange, and collaboration, which should be sufficient to cultivate loyalty among such employees. However, in order to encourage the best possible performance from distributed workers, it is essential for administrators to understand that, regardless of how sophisticated technology may be in opening communication channels, the technology alone does not create a fulfilling work experience (Helms & Raiszadeh, 2002).

Professionals who work from home offices or other distributed sites may experience a sense of social isolation. Marshall, Michaels, and Mulki (2007) argued that "isolation perceptions are formed by the absence of support from co-workers and supervisors, as well as the lack of opportunities for social and emotional interaction with the team" (p. 198). In order to increase opportunity for support and interaction, some universities are investing in sophisticated online professional development and social spaces. It is uncertain how effective these types of online resources will be and the types of faculty who will find the resources effective at reducing their sense of social isolation. Effective networking seems to require—or at least benefit from—periods of informal socialization. This often occurs as a side benefit of face-to-face interaction, but it can also happen in synchronous interactions via audio, video, or immersive conferencing at a distance.

A key question is whether periodically offering remote adjunct faculty face-to-face social meetings strengthens relationships and deepens their sense of commitment to the institution. Just as importantly, will bringing adjunct faculty together deliver a better educational experience to students? In situations where meeting face-to-face on a regular basis is very difficult, the challenge for academic managers is to determine how often they should be creating opportunities for remote faculty to connect with peers and management in a social context or, if this is not possible, to decide how learning institutions can reduce any negative effects of disconnectedness due to adjunct faculty being at a distance.

If meeting in person is not possible, then academic administrators must find ways to create a more personalized rapport with each virtual adjunct faculty and to foster conditions in which social exchanges among remote employees can occur more frequently. Brignall and Van Valey (2005) attempted to clarify that computer-mediated communication (CMC) is not a problem per se. The Internet is simply a tool that can be used in a diversity of ways. The key lies in determining *how* to make use of the medium in order to bond socially with a distributed workforce.

Promoting Connectedness and the Rewards

Eib and Miller (2006), in acknowledging the challenges for distance education universities, suggested that "[c]arefully designed faculty development approaches can create a culture that supports thoughtful focus on teaching, while nurturing the sense of connectedness and collegiality that is vital to continuous innovation and improvement in post-secondary institutions" (Introduction, para 2). One possible approach, proposed by Lowenthal (2008), is to use storytelling in the development of online adjunct faculty. Although asynchronous communication eliminates differences of time and place, allowing many adjunct faculty to attend training and development workshops, it still does not guarantee that content will be engaging or relevant. Lowenthal's solution is to employ storytelling techniques, which add relevance to learning: "By having faculty share their own stories, while also hearing and reading the stories of others, faculty developers can begin to approach faculty development from an additive rather than a deficit or remediation model" (p. 353). Moreover, digital media (e.g., video and audio) have the potential to invite more faculty to participate in sharing their experiences because "[t]he power of the voice is something that cannot be captured the same simply in text" (p. 353). The use of storytelling allows adjunct faculty to share their experiences and their best practices in the classroom with their colleagues. This benefits the adjunct faculty themselves but also the academic program, and most importantly, the students in the adjunct faculty's classes.

Conner (2003) pointed out that individuals working at a distance will put more or less effort into engaging in virtual discussions and understanding how the environment works, depending on their need for affiliation: "A highly educated worker with low affiliation needs may find adapting to a job with high social isolation far easier (even desirable) than a worker with high affiliation needs" (p. 144). Still, as Jackson, Gharavi, and Klobas (2006) explained, a well-managed virtual discussion space has the potential to "increase staff identification with the organization not by increasing admiration for the culture, but by placing the organization in a position of providing the forum for the self-realization of the individual worker through professional expression and relationships" (p. 240).

Levinson (2005) contended that in order to retain online adjunct faculty, institutions must put significant effort into ample and frequent communication using both synchronous and asynchronous methodologies. When interacting with peers, instructors are able to gain insights and information that add to their previous knowledge (Ohlund, Yu, Jannasch-Pennel, & DiGangi, 1999). Asynchronous communication media such as discussion forums and blogs and channels such as Twitter enable instructors across the globe to share and take advantage of new ideas and experiences, independent of time and location. By contrast, in the traditional learning environment, such an opportunity would only arise at academic events attended by instructors from various countries. Moreover, the reach of shared information would only cover a very small percentage of these educators, as clearly no single event could count on the presence of all potential attendees worldwide.

Asynchronous communication tools increase the likelihood that many who otherwise would not have the means to attend international educational events will gain valuable knowledge they can apply in their teaching. By the same token, synchronous technology such as webcasts, although perhaps not attracting the same number of participants because of time constraints, still offers many educators the chance to communicate with peers and exchange knowledge in real time.

Notwithstanding the existence of these effective synchronous and asynchronous means of communication, there are often long periods of time that pass without adjunct faculty having any awareness of the culture, significant events, or changes in policy at the institutions where they teach. And research in this area makes clear that keeping faculty informed and providing feedback on their performance is critical to increasing personal efficacy, reducing feelings of insecurity, and promoting self-esteem (Conner, 2003).

For adjunct faculty, effective social networking supports not only communication around academic and institutional issues but also communication around topics that matter to adjunct faculty personally. Nelson (2002) advocated using technology to "reinforce the human element at work and increase the opportunity to provide meaningful recognition and appreciation to others. . . . Technology can assist in building trust and developing relationships at work as opposed to simply getting more work done faster" (p. 6). Yu and Young (2008) contended that group identity can only result in cooperative behavior once there is a true desire among members of a group to receive others' feedback and help. By providing opportunities for faculty to connect through group networking and collective bonding, institutions can only improve collegiality and friendship (Baker, Redfield, & Tonkin, 2006). "[F]aculty networking and collaborative coaching have the potential to help not only improve faculty attitudes and experiences with online instruction but also produce higher retention and student satisfaction rates" (Baker, Redfield, & Tonkin (2006), "Conclusion" section, para 1). Learning from their peers' knowledge and experience provides inspiration that could only make adjunct faculty better teachers.

Choosing Online or Face-to-Face: Communication Is the Key

It appears, however, that regardless of the channels people choose for communicating with one another—that is, via technology or face-to-face—what is critical is the creation of opportunities for all stakeholders to share their ideas regarding the ongoing improvement of the institution's services and reputation. This in turn will provide students with a more positive and fulfilling experience. As online communication continues to evolve and new capabilities emerge, one fact is undeniable: "Most believe that technology will become ever more interwoven into the fabric of academic life . . . enabling multi-modal teaching, changing curricula and spawning rich forms of online research and collaboration" (Economist Intelligence Unit, 2008, "Introduction" section).

In this context, adjunct faculty will have more and more opportunities to access online educational and reference resources via diverse networking technologies, as the next section of this chapter explores in detail.

NETWORK TECHNOLOGY: ADJUNCT WORK AND LEARNING

Network technologies continue to change the culture of higher education, just as e-mail and online courses have over the past two decades. These constantly changing technologies, available via the Internet, have provided many opportunities for adjunct faculty to become more effective, more connected, and thus more valuable as faculty in the education field.

Successful practitioners in this networked era must develop appropriate levels of network literacy so they can adopt, adapt, and troubleshoot applications they find of compelling value. As important, they must have the ability to critically evaluate new technologies and applications and use their investment of learning time wisely. In addition, each of us benefits from the creation and backing of a helpful social network of colleagues that provides us with appropriate levels of technical and interpersonal support throughout this continuing process of change. We turn now to a model designed to help think about and critically exploit these new, mediated opportunities.

Dron and Anderson (2009) have developed a model that they refer to as a Taxonomy of the Many that categorizes social networking contexts into three domains: Groups, Networks, and Collectives. Each of these contexts is associated with different technologies, applications, learning designs, and outcomes, and a discussion of these affordances defines the next section of this chapter. This model is illustrated in Figure 7.1.

Before moving to a discussion of the affordances of social networking applications, we first discuss the ways in which new technologies provide both opportunity and challenges for adjunct faculty.

Adjunct faculty have multiple reference terms—adjunct, contingent faculty, part-time faculty—individually assigned by each institution of higher education. In their seminal book on "the invisible faculty," Gappa and Leslie (1993) formulated a typology to help define the motivation and lifestyle of adjunct faculty:

    I. *Specialist, Experts, Professionals:* Adjunct faculty work full-time in a profession and teach to remain connected to their professional network.

   II. *Freelancers:* Adjunct faculty have more than one part-time position, or they may even have a full-time position at another college and teach a course for another.

III. *Career Enders:* Adjunct faculty may be near the end or at the end of their career and want to supplement their income or give back to the field and maintain contacts with like professionals.

IV. *Aspiring Academics:* Adjunct faculty may be early in their academic career, looking for experience and the possibility of a full-time academic position.

Adjunct faculty have a professional obligation to use the tools of their profession with high degrees of competence. Unfortunately, unlike their full-time counterparts, they are often not provided with the tools, training, or support to meet these obligations. Thus, adjunct faculty must be more resourceful in acquiring and keeping current with both tools and skills of their profession. Fortunately, the cost of network tools continues to decline and most network

Figure 7.1   Taxonomy of the Many (Dron & Anderson, 2009)

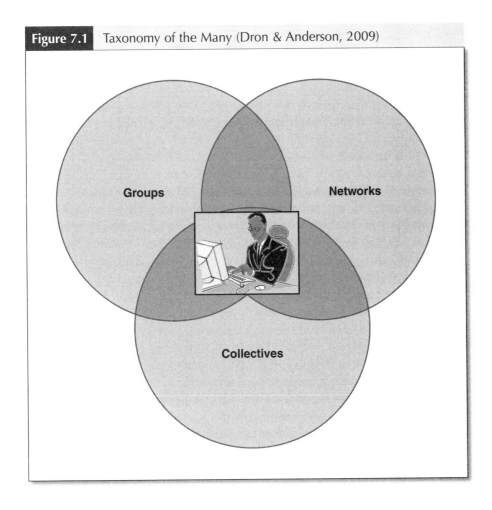

tools are multipurpose enough to find application for personal, entertainment, and vocational applications in addition to their use for adjunct teaching. It is not necessary to own the very latest hardware and software applications or to live on the "bleeding edge" of technological adoption, but neither is it desirable to lapse into a state of technological laggardness.

To meet financial and support restraints, resourceful educators are making more extensive use of open source tools and Web 2.0 applications that utilize applications hosted on the network itself (sometimes referred to as cloud computing), as opposed to those purchased and maintained on a personal computer. For example, the listings of free tools at go2web20.net present over 3,000 applications for education, finance, production, and fun. Specifically, the ever-growing suite of tools (Google apps) offered for free use by Google provides ready and continuous access to most of the productivity tools needed by the resourceful adjunct teacher. But deciding which tools to use can be confusing and no one has time to progress down more than a few blind alleys. To help select appropriate Web 2.0 tools, we next turn back to the Taxonomy of the Many model.

Groups

Groups are a familiar concept to teachers as they form the basis of most formal teaching and learning that takes place at either a distance or on campus. There is a large corpus of research from sociological, psychological, and organizational behavior perspectives documenting the ways in which groups form and evolve to support teaching and learning. The educational research also documents gains in student achievement, persistence, and motivation when learners engage in collaborative and cooperative learning activities (Johnson & Johnson, 1994; Springer, Stanne, & Donovan, 1999). Unfortunately, organization and efficient management of these groups can be challenging and time consuming for the adjunct teacher—especially if the course operates exclusively or in blended online modes—thus, the motivation for the development of numerous group-based communication and information management tools. The most common of these in educational contexts is the suite of tools known as learning management systems (LMS). These systems are either proprietary (Blackboard, Desire to Learn, WebTycho) or open source (Moodle, Sakai) and are usually supported by the educational institution. This institutional support often extends to faculty support classes and training opportunities to enroll in faculty development courses, many of which are taught using the target LMS. Moreover, many of the more popular systems also have extensive online support provided by the manufacturer or various teaching support groups. Gaining mastery of the tools that are included in the LMS suite is a first and critical step for adjunct faculty. Even those who are teaching primarily in a face-to-face format are finding ways in which group LMS tools provide useful extension of the on-campus classroom, creating opportunities for blended learning (Garrison & Kanuka, 2004).

Although groups in education are normally supported through institutional LMS, there are many increasingly wide and diverse sets of group tools that are available outside of the formal institution. These tools provide adjunct faculty with the means to coordinate and create groups and group support materials that are not owned and constrained by a particular institution, and thus they may be used by adjunct faculty for a variety of purposes and in more than a single institution. Examples of these tools include the Google productivity tools, generic Web 2.0 group tools such as wiggio.com, and over 100 Web 2.0 tools categorized as e-learning applications (see go2web20.net/).

Effective management of groups and group tools are necessary skills for all four types of adjunct faculty noted earlier. Perhaps the largest challenge is faced by "freelancers," who may be required to operate more than one set of group LMS tools in the various employment situations in which they find themselves engaged.

Networks

Unlike groups, networks are fluid aggregations of the many that operate to support, entertain, and facilitate communication among widely distributed network members. Networks allow adjunct faculty to be exposed to ideas from outside particular institutional boundaries, thus creating an opportunity for external enrichment. The social scientist Ronald Burt (2005) noted that "people who live in the intersection of social worlds are at higher risk of having good ideas" (p. 90). Burt and other scholars of social capital creation also note that engaging in network activities not only allows networkers to have good ideas, but to share those ideas, thus creating social capital, obligations for reciprocity, and opportunity to altruistically give to one's network communities. Networking opportunities often are supported by a variety of tools, including low cost tools such as e-mail lists (h-net.org/~adjunct/), web sites (adjunctnation.com), and emerging adjunct support networks on social networking sites such as Facebook or LinkedIn. Many adjunct faculty also gain and give support to disciplinary networks that often provide invaluable discipline-related teaching hints, links to both online and face-to-face conferences, recent research results, and employment and service opportunities.

Networks create the social glue that allows individual adjunct faculty members from different disciplinary, geographic, and institutional contexts to explore, inform, and educate each other. Networks thus create a primary means by which adjunct faculty develop and maintain connections with the academy, past and current students, and their discipline.

Effective networking is required for all types of adjunct faculty, as networking leads to currency with subject domain and teaching tools and practices. However, for the aspiring academic type, networking can make a tremendous difference because networks become the course for leads, referrals, and means to build and expend social capital often needed to attain a tenure track academic position.

Collectives

The final domain of the many from Dron and Anderson's (2009) model is collectives, which are aggregations or sets formed from the actions of individuals, bound together by aggregating algorithms that may be as simple as a vote or usage count or as complex as a multilayered, pattern-matching, collaborative filter. Individuals in a collective do not primarily see themselves as members of a Group or connected in a Network, yet their aggregated activities and ideas create collective knowledge. For some kinds of knowledge, the aggregated or averaged behavior of many intelligent agents can be more accurate, complete, or appropriate than that of any one individual (Surowiecki, 2004). Collective knowledge results from the aggregation and processing of the trails left by others as they use the Internet. For example, users who use Cite-U-Like, a popular Web 2.0 tool to manage the academic citations they have read, find individual value by using the tool to generate bibliographic lists. But collectively, these lists can be aggregated to find the most popular citations and those resources cited by particular individuals, groups, or networks, thus creating a new source of knowledge. Although collective tools have only recently been developed, adjunct faculty members are well advised to use them whenever possible to amplify their searching and selection capacity.

APPLICATIONS OF THE TAXONOMY OF THE MANY

The primary applications of the Taxonomy of the Many model relate to means by which these Internet tools can be used to increase productivity, efficiency, and effectiveness of adjunct faculty. Individual time and information management tools, group LMS and classroom facilitation tools, networking and group collaboration tools, and collective aggregations of resources, ideas, and memes all enhance the productivity of adjunct faculty. Many of these tools are also useful in the development and support of student learning activities. The participatory pedagogies that define many types of online and blended learning encourage students to be active creators (in addition to consumers) of knowledge artifacts. For example, the popular Web 2.0 tool Voicethread allows an instructor to begin the voice, video, or text annotation of a wide variety of media objects and set challenging tasks and questions that are answered and debated by learners, thus growing and archiving the multiple perspectives that define critical and constructivist learning. Voicethread can also be used in professional network development as a means to aggregate knowledge from network members on particular problems. For example, a network member may post a question or even a videotape of a common problem and invite members to respond in audio, video, or text format. Again, the responses stay visible for asynchronous use and learning by network members.

Tools and applications are expanding rapidly in all of these areas, and thus limited amounts of time can productively be expended on exploring and exposing oneself to these new opportunities. However, the tools and the Groups, Networks, and Collectives they sustain can and should be employed to filter and find recommendations for tools that may be particularly useful in an individual's disciplinary and institutional context.

A second major set of applications is the capacity of these tools to provide accessible and low-cost professional development activities. Networking with other full-time and adjunct faculty, both within and with other disciplinary perspectives, can provide a wealth of ideas and activities that enhance one's performance and effectiveness as an adjunct faculty member. The development of online conferences promises a means for adjunct faculty (and especially those aspiring to tenure track positions) to participate and gain value from professional academic conferences, even if they are not provided the travel and logistic support to participate face-to-face in these conferences (Siemens, Tittenberger, & Anderson, 2008).

Finally, these tools provide opportunities for adjunct faculty to market their skills, enhance their reputation, and increase their social capital. For those who see their adjunct teaching as a means to full-time academic work or expansion and growth of their professional lives outside of the academy, these tools provide unparalleled opportunity to create and nourish a web presence. Adjunct faculty who take the time to create a web page and add value to online discussions on mailing lists, post reflections and links in blogs and Twitter, and otherwise contribute to knowledge development on the Internet, greatly increase their chance of gaining the attention and acclaim of other academic professionals.

CONCLUSION

In this chapter, we have focused on the challenges that isolation creates for many instructors, especially those who work exclusively online. Dolan's 2009 study demonstrates that solely relying on technology-mediated tools for communication can present challenges in creating and developing adjunct faculty's skills. We thus recommend that institutions develop appropriate—and as yet undiscovered—blends of face-to-face and online communication to ensure that adjunct faculty acquire the opportunities necessary to create effective and satisfied employees.

Finally, we present a model for choosing the communication channels and networking modes that will help adjunct faculty grow their professional competencies, their capacity to work effectively, and their social capital. We trust that, together, the study and model provide guidelines for both adjunct faculty and those administrating programming for reducing the social isolation and disconnectedness that can be associated with adjunct work.

The key points that arise from this chapter include the following:

- Social isolation may be experienced by distant-learning adjunct faculty, and this can have detrimental effects on quality of life, professional development, and teaching effectiveness. It is important for academic institutions to support these instructors by offering them the means to connect with peers and superiors.
- The Internet has been used to create a large variety of professional resources accessible to both face-to-face and online adjunct faculty. These can be and are used by adjunct faculty to exchange best practices and to meet and converse with colleagues, thereby improving their skills, self-realization, and motivation on the job.
- It is in the interest of adjunct faculty, even in the absence of institutional support, to increase their network skills and interests; they will be better able to acquire the resources and contacts that will help them stay current with the tools, key people, and required skills of their profession. Making use of some of the networking avenues presented in this chapter is an important step toward the enrichment of marketable skills as well as a sense of personal fulfillment.

- Networking technologies provide adjunct faculty with many opportunities to become more effective, more in touch with their profession, and thus more valuable as faculty in the education field.
- Determining the best mix of face-to-face and online socialization and networking opportunities will challenge both administrators and adjunct faculty as they learn to work effectively in distributed contexts, with pervasive access to online connectivity.

REFERENCES

Baker, J. D., Redfield, K. L., & Tonkin, S. (2006). Collaborative coaching and networking for online instructors. *Online Journal of Distance Learning Administration, 9*(4). Retrieved November 26, 2007, from http://www.westga.edu/~distance/ojdla/winter94/baker94.htm

Brignall, T. W. III, & Van Valey, T. (2005). The impact of Internet communications on social interaction. *Sociological Spectrum, 25*(3). Retrieved November 26, 2007, from InformaWorld database.

Brindley, J. E., Zawacki, O., & Roberts, J. (2003). Support services for online faculty: The provider's and the users' perspectives. In U. Bernath & E. Rubin (Eds.), *Reflections on teaching and learning in an online master program—A case study* (pp. 137–165). Oldenburg, Germany: Bibliotheks und Informationssystem der Universität Oldenburg.

Burt, R. (2005). *Brokerage and closure: An introduction to social capital.* Retrieved January 2, 2008, from http://books.google.com/books?hl=en&lr=&id=kuJb4H_ABq0C&oi=fnd&pg=PA1&dq=Brokerage+and+Closure&ots=xRVMC20wCY&sig=tWxm4nFtIuRvLhoehL4tpClDdCA#PPP1,M1

Camblin, L. Jr., & Steger, J. A. (2000). Rethinking faculty development. *Higher Education, 39*(1). Retrieved, November 24, 2007, from JSTOR—Journal Storage database.

Conner, D. S. (2003). Social comparison in virtual work environments: An examination of contemporary referent selection. *Journal of Occupational and Organizational Psychology, 76,* 133–147. Retrieved November 16, 2008, from ProQuest database.

Dolan, V. (2009). *The isolation of online faculty and its impact on their performance.* Unpublished master's thesis, Athabasca University, Athabasca, Alberta, Canada.

Dron, J., & Anderson, T. (2009). How the crowd can teach. In S. Hatzipanagos & S. Warburton (Eds.), *Handbook of research on social software and developing community ontologies* (pp. 1–17). Hershey, PA: IGI Global Information Science.

Economist Intelligence Unit. (2008). *The future of higher education: How technology will shape learning.* Retrieved July 8, 2009, from http://www.nmc.org/pdf/Future-of-Higher-Ed-(NMC).pdf

Eib, B. J., & Miller, P. (2006). Faculty development as community building. *International Review of Research in Open and Distance Learning, 7*(2). Retrieved November 20, 2007, from http://www.irrodl.org/index.php/irrodl/rt/metadata/299/639

Gappa, J. M., & Leslie, D. W. (1993). *The invisible faculty: Improving the status of part-timers in higher education.* San Francisco: Jossey-Bass.

Garrison, D. R., & Kanuka, H. (2004). Blended learning: Uncovering its transformative potential in higher education. *Internet and Higher Education, 7*(2), 95–105.

Gordon, M. (2003). *Part-time faculty in community colleges: The jury is still out* (Report No. JC 030 083). Clearwater, FL: St. Petersburg College. (ERIC Document Reproduction Service No. ED472020)

Helms, M. M., & Raizadeh, F. M. E. (2002). Virtual offices: Understanding and managing what you cannot see. *Work Study, 51*(5). Retrieved November 25, 2007, from Ingenta Connect database.

Jackson, P., Gharavi, H., & Klobas, J. (2006). Technologies of the self: Virtual work and the inner panopticon. *Information Technology & People, 19*(3), 219–243. Retrieved December 1, 2008, from Emerald Insight database.

Johnson, D., & Johnson, T. (1994). *Learning together and alone: Cooperative, competitive, and individualistic learning.* Toronto, Ontario, Canada: Allyn & Bacon.

Levinson, D. L. (2005). What do adjunct faculty want? *Community College Week 18*(5). Retrieved October 6, 2005, from EBSCOhost database.

Lowenthal, P. R. (2008). Online faculty development and storytelling: An unlikely solution to improve teacher quality. *MERLOT Journal of Online Learning and Teaching, 4*(3). Retrieved July 13, 2009, from http://jolt.merlot.org/vo14n03/lowenthal_0908.pdf.

Marshall, G. W., Michaels, C. E., & Mulki, J. P. (2007). Workplace isolation: Exploring the construct and its measurement. *Psychology & Marketing, 24*(3). Retrieved November 20, 2007, from InterScience Wiley database.

Nelson, B. (2002). *Managing virtual employees* (in Nelson Motivation online store). Retrieved January 6, 2009, from http://nelson-motivation.stores.yahoo.net/maviem.html

Ohlund, B., Yu, C. H., Jannasch-Pennel, A., & DiGangi, S. (1999). *Impact of asynchronous and synchronous internet-based communication on collaboration and performance among K-12 teachers.* Retrieved July 8, 2009, from http://www.creative-wisdom.com/pub/AERA1999/collaboration.html

Siemens, G., Tittenberger, P., & Anderson, T. (2008). Conference connections: Rewiring the circuit. *EDUCAUSE Review, 43*(2), 14–28. Retrieved November 24, 2009, from http://connect.educause.edu/Library/EDUCAUSE+Review/ConferenceConnections Rewi/46312

Springer, L., Stanne, M., & Donovan, S. (1999). Effects of small-group learning on undergraduates in science, mathematics, engineering and technology: A meta-analysis. *Review of Educational Research, 16*(1), 21–51.

Surowiecki, J. (2004). *The wisdom of crowds.* London: Little, Brown.

Yu, C., & Young, M. (2008). The virtual group identification process: A virtual educational community case. *CyberPsychology & Behavior, 11*(1), 87–90. Retrieved October 20, 2008, from EBSCOhost database.

Appendix A

Administrative and Program Details to Consider Before the Term Begins

Program Administration

_____ Do you have a copy of your contract signed by the provost or academic dean indicating responsibilities and payment?

_____ What are the date, time, and place of your class meetings? Have you prearranged any scheduling conflicts or makeup classes?

_____ Do you have copies of requisite university adjunct or faculty handbooks plus the university's academic guidelines and policies?

_____ Have you spoken with your university contact? Do you know how to obtain whatever support you will need?

_____ Have you obtained your university ID?

Class Details

_____ Where is the classroom located, and what parking is available? Have you obtained any necessary permits?

_____ Have you visited your classroom? Will you need to rearrange anything to accommodate your teaching methods?

_____ Have you addressed personal safety concerns for yourself and the students both coming to and going from class?

_____ Have accommodations been made both in the building and in the classroom for all students?

_____ Do you know how to contact safety and security personnel in the event of an emergency?

_____ Where is the library (or lab) located, and what are the hours of operation?

_____ Have you accessed your electronic course information? Are you able to post information for students?

_____ Have you activated the course to enable student access and capability?

Student Administration

_____ Do you have a general knowledge of registration procedures and add/drop procedures?

_____ Have you been given a class roster or do you have electronic access to one? Have you confirmed actual enrollment information?

_____ Have you been given information regarding the university's grading system and procedures, especially the deadline when final grades are due and how to submit them?

_____ Are you aware of the procedures and expectations for teaching evaluations?

Adjunct Support

_____ Have you made arrangements for any instructional media materials you will require?

_____ Are there any provisions for administrative support? Do you know how to arrange for them?

_____ Are you familiar with the university's library and the resources available pertaining to your subject? Will the library offer you or your students assistance with research? Do you know the procedure for placing materials on reserve?

_____ Have you found contact information and procedures for electronic support of your online course activities?

Appendix B

Checklist for Group Facilitation

Leader Responsibilities

_____ 1. **Arranges seating of participants** so that everyone can see and hear each other.

_____ 2. **States and confirms the agenda.** Obtains answers to the following:
   a. What is the objective of this discussion?
   b. How much time should be spent on each topic?

_____ 3. **States and/or confirms "ground rules" to be followed. Typical Ground Rules for Group Discussion:**
   a. All points of view will be accepted and posted: criticism (evaluation) is ruled out until later.
   b. Interruptions will be "gatekept."
   c. Silence is okay; one needs time to think.
   d. Disagreement is okay as long as it's about ideas, not personalities.
   e. Evaluation of the content and the process comes last.

_____ 4. **Elicits ideas, opinions, and feelings.** Uses recognition, silence, or coaxing, or some combination, to encourage participation. "What do you think about the topic?"

_____ 5. **Posts and confirms key points generated.** List publicly brief summaries of what has been said. Quickly prints a summary statement of what has been said (in own words) and inquires, "Is this correct?"

_____ 6. **Elicits clarification or elaboration.** Asks for examples or illustrations. "Could you give us an example or illustration or help us understand?"

_____ 7. **Recognizes or encourages contributions.** Listens attentively to others' ideas. Reinforces them by adding own ideas or approves them verbally or nonverbally. Uses a nod of the head, a smile, or says, "That's an interesting point."

_____ 8. **States or reflects feelings.** Describes own concerns or feelings about what is happening or restates what he or she thinks others are feeling and asks for confirmation. "It seems to me that we're confused. Is that true? Remember the topic we're discussing is . . ."

_____ 9. **Gatekeeps.** Asks someone to hold off introducing a new topic while another is being discussed; intervenes to prevent people from talking at the same time. "Hold it! Jane, please finish what you were saying. Then we'll get to you, Sam."

_____10. **Tests consensus.** Checks with others to see if they agree with points made or with conclusions stated or to see if everyone is ready to proceed to another topic, issue, or step in problem-solving sequence. "Are there any more ideas about this topic? Are we ready to evaluate or analyze what it means now?"

_____11. **Summarizes.** Pulls together related ideas; tries to draw conclusion. "Let's see, from what's been posted, it seems that we agree that . . ."

_____12. **Analyzes, evaluates.** Asks "Why?" about what has been posted; inquires about supporting assumptions, values, and facts. "Why do you think you felt this way about this topic?"

_____13. **Derives principles or generalizations.** Guides others into either discovering basic principles or transferring conclusions to new settings. "What basic principles seem to be at work here? How does this apply to your field"

Participant Responsibilities (in addition to assisting with the above)

_____14. **Gives information or opinions.** Offers facts or generalizations; makes suggestions honestly, forcefully, and spontaneously. "Here's what I see as the key point of . . . ."

_____15. **Clarifies or elaborates.** Clears up confusion by restating (in his or her own words) what someone else has said or by asking for or giving examples or illustrations. "Let me see if I understand. Is this what you're trying to say?"

_____16. **Accepts others' ideas** or disagreements as ideas to be explored, not personal attacks. Looks for a positive side. "You certainly see things differently. But that's interesting. Let's see . . . ."

_____17. **Ignores aggressiveness**, attempts to impress, and competitive behavior, or points out their dysfunctional and counterproductive consequences. "When people dominate the discussion, I feel frustrated and soon 'tune out.'"

Appendix C

Sample Lesson Plan

Shakespeare Via the Internet

An Educator's Reference Desk Lesson Plan

Submitted by: XXXXXXXXX

E-mail: XXXXXXXXXXXXX

School/University/Affiliation: XXXXXXXXXXXXXXXX

Date: XXX

College Level: Freshman English

Subject(s):

- Computer Science

Description: This lesson serves to develop students' Internet skills in researching a familiar topic. The lesson also serves to reinforce knowledge acquired about the topic.

Goals: The students will be able to

- Explain why Shakespeare is so popular and important
- Appreciate the use of language, become comfortable with reading it, and understand how it enhances the readings

Objective(s): The students will be able to

1. Gain experience in theater and public speaking

2. Recognize how Shakespeare builds his characters and analyze their motives

3. Develop their creative writing skills

4. Become more acquainted with the computer by finding information about Shakespeare on the World Wide Web

5. Type their play, e-mail ideas to group members, create a presentation on the World Wide Web, and finally create a class web page

Materials:

- Shakespeare book
- Handout for group instruction

Procedure:

Activities: Handout already on desk

a. Attention getter

On board—September 27, 1594

"Welcome to the London Theatre! You have just been selected as the talented actors and actresses to perform one of the plays by the wonderful new playwright William Shakespeare."

b. Instructions

- Two plays are *Much Ado About Nothing* and *Romeo and Juliet*—both we have read in class.
- You will be working in groups for this activity, but you will be doing very little interaction face to face with your group for the first few days.
- You will e-mail ideas to your group members while you are searching the World Wide Web for information on Shakespeare, his plays, his life, and so on.

- Be sure to e-mail your group members with links to the great web pages that you find.
- After obtaining the e-mail addresses of your group members, e-mail back and forth regarding the following:

1. Pick one act that your group will perform for this class.

2. Decide who plays each character.

   - Be sure to pick the person who can best represent each character.
   - The purpose of this is to recognize the distinguishing qualities of each character and attempt to portray these qualities in your chosen act.

3. Create a new ending for the scene to work on creative writing skills.

   - This is what will be acted out in class.
   - Be sure to keep the characters' personalities intact.

4. Keep these notes in mind regarding evaluation.

   - I will grade you on how well you seem to understand the characters through the acting out of the scene and by how well you can keep the personality the same in the new ending.
   - I will also grade you on your imaginative ending.
   - You will be graded on how well you keep on task.

   In addition

   - Each group will evaluate another group on character understanding and creativity. I will grade you on your evaluation of another group.
   - You will complete a self-evaluation after you have performed your act.

All of the above activities should take about 15 minutes.

c. Separation into groups

   - Raise hands to decide who goes in each group. Allow students to decide which play they would like to be in, putting about five people in each group.
   - This will take about 5 to 10 minutes.

d. Assignment for the day

   - By the end of the class period each person should turn in
     1. A typed paper with the names of group members and their e-mail addresses

2. As many web addresses as you found today on Shakespeare, ranking them from the best to the worst and tell why

3. Intended act of performance

4. Who plays what character

5. Ideas for new endings

- We will work on this project for one week and perform it beginning next Monday.

This activity should take the remainder of class time.

For disabled students

All students can participate in this activity. If moving around and acting is difficult for one person, he or she can have another part as something a bit less mobile. If speaking is the problem, there are parts with no speaking involved. Any problem that is encountered can be taken care of.

Being that this is a group activity, everyone will be able to work together and produce a quality performance; try to involve everyone.

Shakespeare

We have read two of Shakespeare's plays: *Much Ado About Nothing* and *Romeo and Juliet.*

Your objective

To act out one act from either play, analyzing the characters' motives. But rather than just doing standard Shakespeare, your group will create a new and creative ending for the act.

- While e-mailing between your group members

  1. Pick one act that your group will perform for this class.

  2. Decide who plays each character.

- Be sure to pick the person who can best represent each character.
- The purpose of this is to recognize the distinguishing qualities of each character and attempt to portray these qualities in your chosen act.

  3. Create a new ending for the scene to work on creative writing skills.

- This is what will be acted out in class.
- Be sure to keep the characters' personalities intact.

Timeline

Today:	E-mail group members to begin getting organized (an assignment will be given in class).
Tuesday:	Work on this project in your groups using the word processor to type your ideas. Each group member must use the computer for the same amount of time.
Wednesday:	We will discuss group ideas with the rest of the class. Each group is responsible for a 2–3 minute computer-based presentation of its ideas on this assignment this far.
Thursday:	Writer of the Week.
Friday:	Final touches, practice acting.
Monday:	Begin performances.
Tuesday:	Performances.
Wednesday:	Guest speaker, school computer specialist Mr. Carpenter, will teach us how to create a web page and why it is important.
Thursday:	Begin creating a web page that contains all of the plays that were written by this class.

Be as creative as you can with this. Have fun with it. Feel free to use props, music, or anything else you can think of to make your performance better.

If your group needs help with this project, I will be available after school until 4:30, before school beginning at 7:00, during 5th period, and of course during class. Do not feel bad about asking for help!

Assessment:

1. Teacher Evaluation

   Students will be graded on the following:

   a. How well they understand the characters through the acting out of the scene
   b. How well they can keep the personality the same in the new ending
   c. How imaginative their ending is
   d. How well they can keep on task

2. Peer Evaluations

   a. Each group will evaluate another group on character understanding and creativity. I will grade you on your evaluation of another group.

   b. Each student will complete a self-evaluation on himself or herself and
      on his or her group after performing the act.

(Because students will be evaluated by their group members, it would be a
good idea if everyone in the group participated.)

Useful Internet Resources:

- The Shakespeare Web: http://www.shakespeare.com/
- Shakespeare Oxford Society Homepage: http://www.shakespeare-oxford.com/
- William Shakespeare and the Internet: http://shakespeare.palomar.edu/

Appendix D

Course Syllabus

University
Course Syllabus

Course Number MGT 515	Course Title Team Development and Performance

Fall Semester	Spring Semester	Summer Semester xxx	Year 2009

Name of Instructor **Dr. XXXXXXXXX**

Meeting Day, Time, and Room Number Room: TBD; Time: 9 am–4:30 pm May 30, June 6, June 20, June 27 July 11, July 25
Final Exam Day, Time, and Room Number TBD

Office Hours
By appointment

E-mail: xxxxx@marymount.edu
Office: xxxxxxx
Phone:
Marymount: xxx-xxx-xxxx
Home office: xxx-xxx-xxxx

1. Broad Purpose of Course

The long dominant organizational model of competitive, individual works has changed drastically in the past 20 years, replaced with a team-based, collaborative model. Driven by new management models, quality, information technology, emotional intelligence, and the growing popularity of team coaching, workers are now expected to function, formally or informally, as intact work groups or teams. This course combines current theories of team development and performance with the practice of team facilitation and coaching. It is intended to help managers and specialists become more competent in understanding, developing, and coaching teams.

2. Course Objectives

Upon successful completion of this course, you should be able to do the following:

- Discuss theories of team development and dynamics, and relate these theories to practice.
- Discuss how the components of emotional and social intelligence contribute to team performance.
- Given illustrative problems and scenarios, diagnose and choose appropriate interventions for group problem resolution.
- Effectively demonstrate effective group facilitation skills and strategies.
- Understand and apply a data collection method for assessing team performance, analyze and summarize that data, feed it back to the team or a team representative, and mutually plan an appropriate development or performance strategy.
- Conduct a graduate level literature review on an area of team development and performance.

Teaching Method

Given the nature of this content, this will be a highly experiential course. Much of the class will be devoted to a range of adult, team-based learning methods. These include interactive discussions, participant skill development in teams, role play, assessments, case studies, video, and presentations.

3. Assignments and Grading Policy

Assignment 1 (25%)

Class Participation and Practice Facilitation

This class meets over six Saturdays and is heavily experiential. You are expected to attend every class unless you discuss it with me in advance. Under no circumstances will a student be allowed to miss more than one Saturday class. A significant portion of the class participation is oriented toward preparing the student to demonstrate facilitation skills in a class activity. Therefore, it is important that you be present to learn and practice the drills to prepare you for this activity. In addition, you will be taking the Team Emotional and Social Intelligence Survey (TESI), an online team emotional intelligence assessment. It is essential that you be in class to get the instructions for this assessment and for getting the feedback. If you are absent, you must get the instructions and feedback from another student.

Assignment 2 (50%)

Group Team Assessment Project

- Work in teams of two to four to accomplish this assignment.
- Identify a real performing team. The team can be from your workplace, place of worship, or community.
- Contract with the team (first preference), team leader, or other contact to conduct an assessment of the team. In discussions with the team or contact, determine what kind of data collection method to use.
- Conduct the data collection, assuring anonymity but not confidentiality.
- Analyze and summarize the data into useable and actionable themes. Determine appropriate recommendations for team interventions.
- Conduct a feedback meeting with the team and or contact. Plan with the team what next steps should be.

- Write a report (5–10 pp.) of these steps for the instructor. Include a copy of the data collection instrument or assessment and the data summary. Do not include the raw data. A grading point evaluation sheet will be distributed separately.

Assignment 3 (25%)

Individual Literature Review and Small-Group Presentation

Each student will choose a topic related to the subject matter of the course, research the topic, and prepare a literature review for distribution in class. Topics selected may include but are not limited to the following:

- Stages of group development
- Emotional Intelligence in teams
- Team coaching
- Team facilitation skills and models
- Team data collection methods
- Facilitative roles
- Models of group decision making
- Self-managed work teams
- Evaluating team performance
- Team leading versus team coaching
- Managing virtual teams
- Team-based organizations—the latest research
- Team assessment tools
- Diversity issues in teams
- Managing conflict in teams
- Appreciative Inquiry application in teams
- Personality type and teams
- Teams and culture

You should make enough copies of your literature review for everyone in the class. Your literature review should cover 10 to 15 articles or books. You are not expected to read each book. You should read several synopses and book reviews to be able to discuss them with the class. However, you should make attempts to read the articles in your literature review. You will describe your literature review in small groups. You will also facilitate a brief exercise of your choosing in your small group that pertains to your literature review. This exercise may be a skill development exercise, an assessment, a game, a role-play, a facilitated discussion, and so forth. A grading point evaluation sheet will be distributed separately.

4. Grade-Point Scale

To attain a grade of:	The minimum point value is:
A	93
A-	90
B+	87
B	84
B-	80
C+	77
C	75
C-	72

5. Class Schedule

Session	Topics
May 30	• Introductions • Course overview and requirements • Course projects: Discussion and selection • Groups and teams—overview of a working model • Instructions on TESI • Facilitation: Basics • Tools and techniques
June 6	• TESI debrief and discussion • Emotional Intelligence in teams • Data collection, analysis, and feedback in teams • Practice in team assessment • Team building activity and debrief
June 20	• Guest speaker: Sticky Wall • Facilitation and discussion or applications • Facilitation models and demonstrations • Video conflict in teams • Facilitating conflict and disagreement

(Continued)

(Continued)

Session	Topics
June 27	• Update and discussion on assignment progress • Choosing appropriate team interventions • Practice facilitation (Assignment 1)
July 11	• Team norms: Unwritten and written • Activity on team norms • Guest speaker: Action learning in teams • Update on assignments, individual research, consultation with instructor
July 25	• Small-group sharing of literature reviews (Assignment 3) • Large-group informal sharing and discussion of Assignment 2 • Wrap-up; turn in all assignments and lessons learned

6. Texts

Required

- Hughes, Marcia, & Terrell, James Bradford. (2007). *The Emotionally Intelligent Team.* San Francisco: Jossey-Bass.
- Team Emotional and Social Intelligence Survey (TESI). Published by Collaborative Growth. Price TBD after first class.

7. References and Suggested Readings

There are myriad, pertinent texts and journal articles available. Some select sources follow.

Group Facilitation Listserve: Send an email message to Listserv@albany.edu. In the body of the message, type "subscribe grp-facl your name." Do not include any other text or signature in your message.

Bradford, L. P. (1978). *Group development.* San Diego, CA: Pfeiffer.

Deeprose, D. (1995). *The team coach.* New York: AMACOM.

Doyle, M., & Straus, D. (1993). *How to make meetings work.* New York: Berkley.

Francis, D., & Young, D. (1992). *Improving work groups.* San Diego, CA: Pfeiffer.

Friend, J., & Hickling, A. (1988). *Planning under pressure.* New York: Pergamon Press.

Goodman, P., & Wright, G. (1991). *Decision analysis for management judgment.* New York: John Wiley.

Goodman, P. S., & Associates. (1986). *Designing effective work groups.* San Francisco: Jossey-Bass.

Guzzo, R. A., Salsa, E., & Associates. (1995). *Team effectiveness and decision making in organizations.* San Francisco: Jossey-Bass.

Hackman, J. R. (2002). *Leading teams: Setting the stage for great performances.* Boston: Harvard Business School Press.

Hughes, M., Thompson, H. L., & Terrell, J. B. (Eds.). (2009). *Handbook for developing emotional and social intelligence.* San Francisco: Pfeiffer.

Janis, I. L., & Mann, L. (1977). *Decision making.* New York: The Free Press.

Katzenbach, J., & Smith, D. (1999). *The wisdom of teams.* New York: Harper.

Kayser, T. A. (1990). *Mining group gold.* El Segundo, CA: Serif Publishing.

Krueger, R. A. (1988). *Focus groups.* Newbury Park, CA: Sage.

Mosvick, R. K., & Nelson, R. B. (1987). *We've got to start meeting like this.* Glenview, IL: Scott, Foresman.

Nutt, P. C. (2002). *Why decisions fail.* San Francisco: Berrett-Loehler.

Reddy, W. B. (1994). *Intervention skills: Process consultation for small groups and teams.* San Diego, CA: Pfeiffer.

Russo, J. E., & Schoemaker, P. J. (1989). *Decision traps.* New York: Fireside.

Salas, E., Bowers, C., & Edens, E. (Eds.). (2001). *Improving teamwork in organizations.* Mahwah, NJ: Lawrence Erlbaum.

Schwarz, R. M. (2002). *The skilled facilitator—Practical wisdom for developing effective groups* (2nd ed.). San Francisco: Jossey-Bass.

Yeatts, D. E., & Hyten, C. (1998). *High-Performance self-managed work teams.* Thousand Oaks, CA: Sage.

8. University Honor Pledge

As a member of the University community, I agree to uphold the principles of honor set forth by this community, to defend these principles against abuse or misuse, and to abide by the regulations of the university.

9. Disability Accommodation Statement

Special needs and accommodations: Please address with the instructor any special problems or needs at the beginning of the semester. Those seeking accommodations based on disabilities should obtain a Faculty Contact Sheet from the Disability Support Services (DSS) office located on the Main Campus.

10. Access to Student Work

Copies of your work in this course, including copies of any submitted papers and your portfolios, may be kept on file for institutional research, assessment, and accreditation purposes. All work used for these purposes will be submitted anonymously.

Appendix E

Suggested Readings and/or Web Site URLs

For Faculty

Selected Web Site Resources

- Carnegie Mellon Eberly Center for Teaching Excellence and Office of Technology for Education: http://www.cmu.edu/teaching/ (see especially the page on "assessment tools")
- DePaul Teaching Commons: http://teachingcommons.depaul.edu (see especially the page on "what we can do with what we learn from assessment")
- Vanderbilt Center for Teaching: http://www.vanderbilt.edu (see especially the pages on interpreting and acting on student ratings and midterm student feedback data)
- Cornell University: http://www.cte.cornell.edu/campus/teach/faculty/TeachingMaterials.html
- Honolulu Community College: http://honolulu.hawaii.edu/intranet/committees/FacDevCom/guidebk/teachtip/develsyl.htm
- Teach Philosophy 101: http://www.teachphilosophy101.org/Default.aspx?tabid=90
- University of Delaware: http://cte.udel.edu/
- University of Michigan: http://www.crlt.umich.edu/gsis/P2_1.php
- University of Minnesota: http://www1.umn.edu/ohr/teachlearn/tutorials/syllabus/what/index.html
- University of West Florida: http://uwf.edu/cutla/assessstudent.cfm

Conferences and Organizations

- International Society for the Scholarship of Teaching and Learning: http://www.issotl.org
- Lilly Conference on College Teaching: http://www.units.muohio.edu/lillycon/
- Teaching Professor Conference: http://www.teachingprofessor.com/

Teaching Blogs

- Tomorrow's Professor: http://amps-tools.mit.edu/tomprofblog/

For Deans, Chairs, and Coordinators of Adjunct Faculty Affairs

Books

Baron-Nixon, L. (2007). *Connecting non full-time faculty to institutional mission: A guidebook for college/university administrators and faculty developers.* Sterling, VA: Stylus Publishing.

Gillespie, K. H., Hilsen, L. R., & Wadsworth, E. C. (2002). *A guide to faculty development: Practical advice, examples, and resources.* Bolton, MA: Anker.

Seldin, P., & Associates. (1995). *Improving college teaching.* Bolton, MA: Anker.

Sorcinelli, M. D., Austin, A. E., Eddy, P. L., & Beach, A. L. (2006). *Creating the future of faculty development: Learning from the past, understanding the present.* Bolton, MA: Bolton.

Web Sites

- Association of American Colleges and Universities: http://www.aacu.org/
- DePaul Teaching Commons: http://teachingcommons.depaul.edu/
- POD (Professional and Organizational Development Network in Higher Education): http://www.podnetwork.org/

Index

NOTE: In page references, f indicates figures and t indicates tables.

About the Editors

Lorri E. Cooper is associate professor and director of the MS in Management program at Marymount University in Arlington, VA. She teaches courses in leadership, managing innovation, and the management capstone and chairs the university's Graduate Studies Committee. Her research and writing focus on leadership development, particularly for practicing managers, management education, and how principles of design can effectively enhance and influence leadership practices. She earned a masters degree at Vanderbilt University and her doctorate degree at the University of Virginia, where she minored in leadership studies and wrote her dissertation on leadership development for private college presidents and governing boards. During her time at the University of Virginia, she served as a research associate and then as an administrative director at the Darden Graduate School of Business Administration. Prior to her academic career, she worked in management consulting with banking and real estate industries in the Washington, D.C., metropolitan area.

Bryan A. Booth is professor and executive director of the Doctor of Management program at University of Maryland University College (UMUC) in Adelphi, MD. In that role he provides leadership and manages the 48-credit, part-time, cohort-based, doctorate program for over 350 students. He earned his PhD in organizational behavior, with minors in anthropology and human resources, from the Industrial and Labor Relations School at Cornell University. In addition, he earned a certificate in Management and Leadership in Education from Harvard's Graduate School of Education. His research and application interests include team development, especially among faculty; emergent leadership; and multimethod collaboration in the classroom. He has training experience in developing the multicultural classroom and cross-cultural communication. Prior to joining UMUC, he taught Organizational Behavior, Labor Relations, and International Business at Shippensburg University, where he also directed the International Management major.

About the Contributors

Terry D. Anderson is professor and Canada Research Chair in Distance Education at Athabasca University, Canada's Open University, where he teaches educational technology courses in the Master's and Doctorate of Distance Education programs. He is active in provincial, national, and international distance education associations, and his widely published research has focused on interaction and its use and impact in distance education. Anderson is the director of CIDER, the Canadian institute for Distance Education Research (http://cider.athabascau.ca), and the editor of the *International Review of Research on Distance and Open Learning* (http://www.irrodl.org). His most recent edited book, *The Theory and Practice of Online Learning* (2nd ed.), was the winner of the 2009 Charles E. Wedemeyer Award for the outstanding book of 2008, awarded by the Distance Learning Community of Practice of the University Continuing Education Association. His blog, the "Virtual Canuck," is accessible at http://terrya.edublogs.org.

Jodi R. Cressman is founding director, Center of Teaching and Learning Excellence at Dominican University in River Forest, IL. In that role, she supports both full-time and adjunct faculty in evaluating and improving their teaching and engaging in the scholarship of teaching and learning. She also serves as associate professor of English, with a primary scholarly interest in autobiography. Before coming to Dominican, Jodi taught English and directed the Office for Teaching, Learning and Assessment at DePaul University. Jodi has published and presented on higher education topics such as assessing understanding and critical thinking, faculty theories of learning, and increasing student engagement. She has also served as an assessment mentor for the Higher Learning Commission. She earned her MA and PhD from Emory University.

Vera L. B. Dolan holds a master's degree in distance education from Athabasca University, where her thesis research focused on the factors that drive motivation and loyalty in online faculty, work that was recognized by a graduate award from the Canadian Network for Innovation in Education (CNIE). She is continuing these investigations at the doctoral level, focusing on faculty training and the delivery and improvement of online education. Following completion of an undergraduate degree in communications at PUC de São Paulo, Dolan began her professional career in media communications and human resources at Citibank/MasterCard Brazil. Upon moving to Canada, she completed the postgraduate program in Human Resources Management at Seneca College and worked as a cross-cultural trainer with executives from a wide range of organizations, including Exxon/Imperial Oil, McKinsey, Warner-Lambert, and the Government of Canada.

Susanne Bruno Ninassi is assistant professor and program director for Business Law, Paralegal Studies, and Legal Administration programs at Marymount University in Arlington, VA. Serving in this capacity, she is responsible for leading the programs, advising both undergraduate and graduate students, managing program faculty, and teaching several courses, including the following: Introduction for the Legal System, Civil Litigation, Business Law I and II, and Paralegal Internship. In addition to serving on academic panels and boards, she is a member of the university's Academic Integrity Committee. She has addressed professional conferences and published a number of papers concerning her academic interests in ethics in health care and paralegal education and development. Before coming to Marymount, she earned her JD at the University of Baltimore School of Law and practiced law in the Washington, D.C., metropolitan area, specializing in civil litigation. She is licensed to practice law in Maryland and the District of Columbia.

Cynthia H. Roman is assistant professor of management and director of Human Resource Management programs at Marymount University in Arlington, VA. She also has over 20 years of experience in management consulting, leadership coaching, training, and organization development, and she is managing partner with Strategic Performance Group, a management consulting firm in the Washington, D.C., area. She has coauthored two books on leadership coaching and is currently writing a book on teaching and learning in higher education for the American Society of Training and Development. Before coming to Marymount, Dr. Roman taught at several other universities, including the University of Maryland and the University of North Carolina. She has taught both graduate and undergraduate students, in the classroom and online.

Dr. Roman received her doctoral degree from Virginia Tech and wrote her dissertation on effective instruction in graduate education. Her academic interests are in leadership coaching, learning theory, and instructional methods.

Theodore E. Stone is director of Academic Technology, Office of Information Technology, at University of Maryland University College (UMUC) in Adelphi, MD. In that role, he monitors and evaluates emerging technologies for review and potential inclusion into the University's e-learning suite. As a faculty member at UMUC, Dr. Stone is a professor in the Master of Education program, where he specializes in courses on educational technology and has led the capstone course for the MEd program for several years. Dr. Stone has taught Instructional Design and Educational Technology in the University System of Maryland since 1992. Before coming to UMUC, Dr. Stone was director of Learning Technologies at the University of Maryland School of Nursing, Baltimore. His PhD was earned at the University of Maryland at College Park in the field of Curriculum and Instruction. His academic interests are in faculty development, teaching with technology, consumer informatics, and lifelong learning.

Supporting researchers for more than 40 years

Research methods have always been at the core of SAGE's publishing program. Founder Sara Miller McCune published SAGE's first methods book, *Public Policy Evaluation*, in 1970. Soon after, she launched the *Quantitative Applications in the Social Sciences* series—affectionately known as the "little green books."

Always at the forefront of developing and supporting new approaches in methods, SAGE published early groundbreaking texts and journals in the fields of qualitative methods and evaluation.

Today, more than 40 years and two million little green books later, SAGE continues to push the boundaries with a growing list of more than 1,200 research methods books, journals, and reference works across the social, behavioral, and health sciences. Its imprints—Pine Forge Press, home of innovative textbooks in sociology, and Corwin, publisher of PreK–12 resources for teachers and administrators—broaden SAGE's range of offerings in methods. SAGE further extended its impact in 2008 when it acquired CQ Press and its best-selling and highly respected political science research methods list.

From qualitative, quantitative, and mixed methods to evaluation, SAGE is the essential resource for academics and practitioners looking for the latest methods by leading scholars.

For more information, visit **www.sagepub.com**.